CW00951883

RELISH
WALES

Original recipes from the region's finest chefs

First Published 2011
By Relish Publications
Shield Green Farm, Tritlington,
Northumberland NE61 3DX

ISBN 978-0-9564205-7-2

Publisher: Duncan L Peters
General Manager: Teresa Peters
Marketing and Design: Ria Parkin
Photography: Tim Green
Senior Account Manager: Paul Bamber
Proof Assistants: Jack Bamber, Victoria Mumford
Printed By: Balto Print Ltd, Stratford,
London E15 2TF

RELISH
PUBLICATIONS.CO.UK

Wales Millennium Centre, Bute Place, Cardiff

004 CONTENTS

DESERTS

RESTAURANTS

CONTENTS

DESSERTS	RESTAURANTS	PAGE
Chocolate Ravioli with Cacen Gri	Manorhaus	150-159
Autumn Fruit Jelly with Muscadel Wine and a Cardamom and Vanilla Ice Cream	Mimosa Kitchen and Bar	160-169
Perry Jelly and Summer Fruits with Elderflower Ice Cream	The Newbridge on Usk	170-179
Duo of Soufflés	The Old Rectory	180-189
Cinnamon Biscuit of Apple and Rhubarb with Elderflower Custard	Plas Bodegroes	190-199
Pavlova	The Queen's Head	200-209
Dark Chocolate Ganache, Beetroot, Raspberry, Yoghurt and Apple	Seaview Restaurant with Rooms	210-219
Tart Tatin	Sosban	220-229
Treacle Tart, Toffee Sauce, Clotted Cream	Three Salmons Hotel	230-239
Warm Chocolate Mousse, Doughnuts, Buttermilk Sorbet	Ty Mawr Mansion Country House	240-249
Almond Tart with Prune and Mascarpone Ice Cream	Tyddyn Llan	250-259
Orange and Almond Cake	The Walnut Tree	260-269
Toffee Apple Crumble Knickerbocker Glory	Y Polyn	270-279
Treacle Tart	Ye Olde Bulls Head Inn	280-289

INTRODUCTION
WITH
SHAUN HILL

Shaun Hill started work for Robert Carrier at his eponymous restaurant in Islington in the late sixties. He became Head Chef at the Michelin-starred Capital Hotel in Knightstbridge in the mid seventies before leaving London to work in the countryside, at Gidleigh Park on Dartmoor as head chef for nine years then at his own restaurant the Merchant House in Ludlow for another eleven years. Shaun took over the Walnut Tree in late 2007. He has written four cookery books: The Gidleigh Park Cookery Book, The Merchant House Cookery Book, Vegetable Cookery – for the BBC – and How to Cook Better, which won the Guild of Food Writer Award for Best Cookery Book. He has also published several books on food in Antiquity. Shaun won the AA Guides Chef's Chef of the Year Award, the Egon Ronay Guide Chef of the Year Award, the Catey Award – sort of an industry Oscar - as Chef of the Year and also Restaurateur of the Year.

Wales has always had good produce and a solid base of great home-cooking, but the restaurant scene has been a little slow to catch up. It is a country with a tradition of first-class baking and of sympathetic but not overly fancy treatments of meat, fish and vegetables. This has yielded dishes that reflect the integrity of the produce rather than the vanity of the cook. Perhaps there has been a history in which elaborate use of often expensive and luxurious ingredients may have seemed overindulgent; somehow a touch improper in a country that is rich in poetry and beauty, but traditionally short on disposable income.

All the same, restaurants are now thriving across the country, not just in the urban south, but across the mountains and valleys of rural Wales. We see ourselves partly as ambassadors for the first-rate produce that is reared and grown here. More importantly however, our chefs are keen to show themselves both as skilled and enthusiastic, cooking this produce to its best effect not just in versions of age-old dishes but in more modern takes on the same fine ingredients. These dishes reflect today's tastes and availabilities, and are not just nostalgia for a long-lost past.

Restaurant food is of course entertainment as well as nourishment. Craftsmanship, a deft hand with slicing and chopping, is not the whole story. All of these clever techniques need to be coupled with taste; an idea of which sauces or spices, if any, will turn a fine piece of fish or lamb into an evening's pleasure, that will work well with the wine or beer that might partner it, and how to get this to the diner in perfect condition. The chef should know when the dish is finished and the point when any further touches would make it less rather than more, and in addition the restaurant manager will try to pace the meal so that you enjoy the experience, and are maybe persuaded to try a wine or ale you hadn't thought of.

So, from the Chowns' estimable Plas Bodegroes on the Lleyn Peninsula, past the Webbs' Tyddyn Llan on the borders of Snowdonia, across to the Mansons' Y Polyn in Carmarthen, you will find personally-and individually-run hotels and restaurants which compete with the best nationwide. Of course my hope is that you also find time for Monmouthshire where you at least have only a short drive between restaurants such as the Hardwick or the Crown at Whitebrook, before a final lunch 10 miles before the border with England at perhaps ... the Walnut Tree?

Eat well and enjoy!
Shaun Hill

010
1861

Cross Ash, Abergavenny, South Wales NP7 8PB

0845 388 1861
01873 821 297
www.18-61.co.uk

As chef/proprietor of 1861, which is located in the pretty hamlet of Cross Ash, near Abergavenny, Simon King has made a huge success of the restaurant that he runs alongside his wife, Kate.

Having trained with the Roux Brothers at their famous Waterside Inn Restaurant on the Thames, also worked with the two Michelin-starred chef Martin Blunos for seven years, Simon went on to become head chef at the luxury country house hotel, Llansantffraed Court.

The doors to restaurant 1861 opened just four years ago and now Simon and Kate are proud to hold 2 AA Restaurant Rosettes and to be included in the prestigious Michelin guide.

1861 is run very much as a family business. Kate and Simon live above the restaurant with their two small children, while Kate's father provides all the vegetables from his nearby market garden.

Simon enjoys deliveries from him twice a day, ensuring that the vegetables, salads and herbs are beautifully fresh. He is also a great forager, and his wild garlic risotto, along with his elderflower fritters, have become firm favourites with his guests.

Simon and Kate have built upon their wealth of hotel and restaurant experience to offer the guests at 1861 a gourmet menu that combines fine food with just the right balance of friendly, personal service.

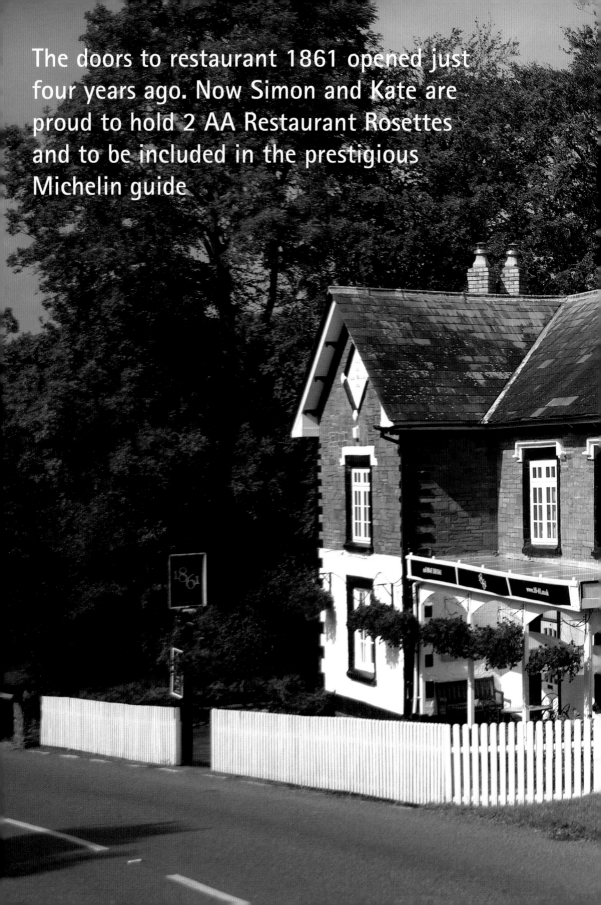

The doors to restaurant 1861 opened just four years ago. Now Simon and Kate are proud to hold 2 AA Restaurant Rosettes and to be included in the prestigious Michelin guide

SEARED SCALLOPS, AUBERGINE CAVIAR, TOMATO COULIS

SERVES 4

Don Cristobal 1492 Torrontes
(Argentina)

Ingredients

2 large courgettes (sliced into ribbons with a
potato peeler)
12 large king scallops
extra virgin olive oil

Aubergine Caviar

1 large aubergine
2 cloves garlic
extra virgin olive oil
lemon juice

Tomato Coulis

450g beef tomatoes
1 onion (chopped into 1cm dice)
1 clove of garlic
extra virgin olive oil

Method

For the aubergine caviar

Split the aubergine in half lengthways then slash the flesh in a
criss-cross fashion and stud with slivers of garlic. Season lightly
and fry in a hot pan with a dash of olive oil until golden brown.
Place the 2 halves back together then wrap them in foil and bake
in a medium oven (180°C) for 30 to 40 minutes until tender.

When cooked, transfer the aubergine to a food processor and
purée until smooth, then adjust the seasoning and add a squeeze
of lemon juice. For an extra smooth puree it can then be pressed
through a sieve. Keep in a warm place until ready to serve.

For the tomato coulis

Sweat the chopped onion and garlic in olive oil until soft and
translucent. Meanwhile, de-seed the tomatoes and roughly chop
the flesh, before adding it to the pan and cook quickly until soft.
Season the coulis with salt and pepper and maybe a little sugar
if desired. Liquidise until smooth then strain the mixture through
a fine sieve and into a small saucepan. Keep warm until ready
to serve.

To serve

Steam the courgette ribbons for a couple of minutes. Pan-fry the
scallops in olive oil in a hot pan for 1 minute on either side, or
until cooked to your liking.

Spoon the aubergine into the base of a cleaned scallop shell or
into a serving bowl. Season the courgettes and arrange neatly
around the aubergine. Place 3 scallops per portion on top of the
aubergine and courgette. Spoon the tomato coulis around the
plate and finally drizzle with a little olive oil.

ROAST RUMP OF LAMB, ROSEMARY JUS

SERVES 4

🍷 *Norton Reserva Malbec*
(Argentina)

Ingredients

4 x 150-200g rumps of lamb (bones removed)
1 bunch rosemary
500g lamb bones (chopped small)
1 onion (diced)
1 carrot (diced)
375ml white wine
1 litre lamb stock
selection of seasonal vegetables

Method

Seal the lamb in a hot pan until golden brown, then place the lamb bones in a roasting tray with the carrots and onions arranging the rumps of lamb on top.

Roast the lamb in a hot oven (200°C) for 15-20 minutes to achieve a medium cooked finish, or until cooked to your liking. Remove the lamb from the oven and keep it in a warm place to rest for 10 minutes.

Remove the lamb bones from the tray and, whilst they are still piping hot, stir in the white wine to deglaze. Bring the pan to the boil and reduce the whole mixture by half. Add the lamb stock and reduce further, until a sauce-like consistency is achieved. Roughly chop the rosemary and add to the sauce, leaving it to infuse for 5 minutes before straining through a fine sieve into a clean saucepan. Bring the sauce to the boil once more. Adjust the seasoning as desired.

To serve

Serve the lamb carved into thin slices along with your favourite seasonal vegetables. Here I have used some creamed potatoes, carrots, beetroot and curly kale. Finally, spoon the sauce over the lamb and serve.

STRAWBERRY VACHERIN

SERVES 4

🍷 *Meinklang Pinot Blanc Ice Wine*
(Austria)

Ingredients

Meringue

2 egg whites
100g caster sugar
2 drops rose extract

Strawberry Sauce

100g strawberries
caster sugar to taste
lemon juice to taste

To Finish

150ml Jersey cream
50g melted chocolate
200g strawberries
12 wild strawberries-optional
strawberry sorbet

Method

For the meringue

Semi whip the egg whites in a clean mixing bowl, then add the caster sugar and continue to whisk until the mix forms soft peaks. Add the rose extract and whip briefly to mix it in. Pipe the meringue into 8 x 8cm circles on greaseproof paper. Bake in the oven on its lowest setting for 2-3 hours until crisp.

For the sauce

Hull and wash the strawberries, then place them into a blender and blend until smooth. Add a little sugar and lemon juice to taste, then blitz again to make sure the sugar is dissolved. Strain the sauce through a sieve and set aside until needed.

To assemble

Hull and wash the strawberries, place them in a bowl and add a tablespoon of the sauce to coat them. Arrange the strawberries neatly around the edges of the meringue bases and spoon the cream into the centre. Place the meringue in the middle of the plate and decorate the remaining area with strawberry sauce. Next place a meringue lid on top. Warm the chocolate over a water bath until it melts, then drizzle some over the meringue lid. Add a scoop of strawberry sorbet on top and finish by decorating with wild strawberries.

020
THE BEAUFORT RAGLAN

High Street, Raglan Village, Monmouthshire NP15 2DY

01291 690 412
www.beaufortraglan.co.uk

There has been an inn on this site, close to medieval Raglan Castle, since the 15th century. Maybe the parliamentary soldiers who 'holed up' here during the civil war knew a thing or two about where to find good food, ale and hospitality.

The current Beaufort has been in the ownership of Eliot and Jana Lewis since 2002. Believing in the maxim of 'good food, good wines and ales, in a relaxed informal atmosphere with bedrooms to match', they have worked to provide an inn which combines the best of the old with every modern convenience. Beams and flagstone floors blend easily with deep leather sofas, open fires and candle light. A south-facing terrace is the perfect place to enjoy this atmosphere while enjoying summer alfresco dining. Bedrooms are individually decorated complete with flat screen televisions and wifi connection.

Food is available throughout; in the traditional lounge bar, a contemporary brasserie, the private dining room, an events suite and a local's 'country bar', depending on the occasion and the diner's individual preference. The kitchen team, led by Paul Webber who returned to this his home county 3 years ago, has set up good relationships with local suppliers to provide food which is not pretentious or fussy, allowing classic favourites to sit alongside a selection of more innovative dishes where clean flavours are key. The seasonal menu changes regularly and the weekly chalkboard reflects the availability of the very best produce. All breads, desserts and ice creams are made in house.

All of this is combined with front of house staff, and includes the owners themselves whom offer a warm welcome, and unfussy but attentive service. This means that for business, pleasure, special occasions, or just a stop for coffee and a chat, the experience at the Beaufort is one to be repeated.

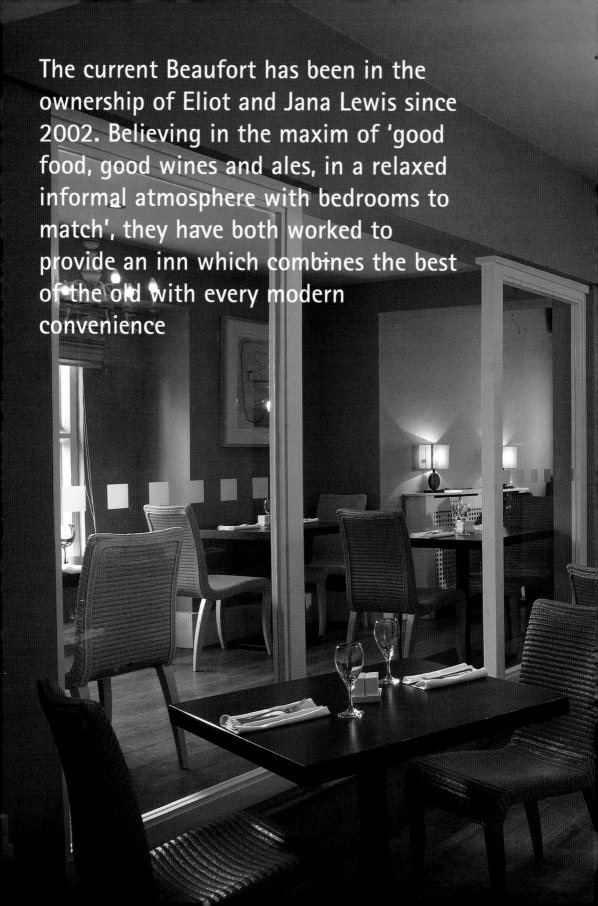

The current Beaufort has been in the ownership of Eliot and Jana Lewis since 2002. Believing in the maxim of 'good food, good wines and ales, in a relaxed informal atmosphere with bedrooms to match', they have both worked to provide an inn which combines the best of the old with every modern convenience

BREAST OF LAMB, POACHED PEAR, PALOISE SAUCE

SERVES 2

*Boomerang Bay Chardonnay, Grant Burge,
South East Australia*

Ingredients

1 breast of lamb (boned, rolled and tied)
3 mint leaves
1 onion (chopped)
50mls red wine
1litre water
1 bay leaf
50g butter

Paloise Sauce

10ml white wine vinegar
1tbsp mint (chopped)
10g shallots (finely diced)
2 egg yolks
125g clarified butter
juice of ½ lemon

Poached Pear

2 medium pears
187ml red wine
125g caster sugar
250ml water

Method

For the lamb

In a thick-bottomed saucepan, seal the lamb completely in the butter, allowing it to brown. Then remove the lamb from the pan and place it in a roasting pan. Deglaze the pan with the red wine, adding the bay leaf, mint, onion and then pour the water over the lamb. Cover the whole roasting pan with foil and cook at 180°C until the lamb is tender. Remove from the oven and leave to rest for 15 minutes.

For the paloise sauce

Combine the vinegar, mint and shallots in a pan and reduce the liquid by half. In a separate bowl, whisk the egg yolks and cooled vinegar reduction over a pan of simmering water until an emulsion is achieved. Removed from the heat and slowly add the clarified butter whilst whisking constantly. Set aside.

For the poached pear

Gently heat the wine and water with the sugar until completely dissolved. Add the pears and simmer gently for 45 minutes or until the pears yield.

To serve

Carve the lamb into 4 even sized pieces and serve alongside a poached pear. Finish with paloise sauce and garnish.

GLOUCESTER OLD SPOT PORK WELLINGTON, BOUDIN NOIR & MUSHROOM DUXELLE, POMME ANNA, CALVADOS REDUCTION

SERVES 2

Chablis – J Moreau et Fils,
Burgundy France

Ingredients

Pork Wellington

380g pork tenderloin (trimmed and cut into 2 pieces)
75g boudin noir
160g chestnut mushrooms
20g butter
1 medium onion
250g puff pastry
1 free range egg
1 clove garlic
2 slices of Parma ham

Pomme Anna

3 large potatoes (peeled and thinly sliced)
3 sage leaves
125g melted butter

Calvados Reduction

20g shallot (finely diced)
150ml calvados
25g butter
75ml veal stock
20g caster sugar

Method

For the pork wellington

Seal each piece of pork fillet in a hot pan and then remove them from the pan to rest. Add the boudin noir, sliced mushrooms and diced onion to the pan and cook, then drain any excess liquid and pulse the mixture in a food processor until roughly chopped. Leave to cool.

Roll each piece of pork fillet along with half of the duxelle in a slice of Parma ham. Roll the pastry until 8mm thick, then divide it into 2 rectangles and wrap one around each piece of pork. Glaze the pastry with beaten egg and cook for 25-30mins in a moderate oven.

For the pomme anna

In a cast iron dish, layer the sliced potatoes with melted butter and sage. Season with salt and pepper. Cover and bake at 200°C for 20 minutes then uncover and continue to bake until the potatoes are golden.

For the calvados reduction

Sweat the shallots in the butter without colouring them, then add the calvados and flame it down. Add the sugar and veal stock and reduce the liquid to half its original volume.

To serve

Assemble as in the picture.

BAILEYS CRÈME BRÛLÉE

SERVES 6

Errazuriz Late Harvest Sauvignon Blanc,
Casablanca Valley

Method

Combine the egg yolks and caster sugar in a bowl. Heat the cream and baileys liqueur in a pan until just below boiling, then remove them from the heat and strain the hot cream onto the egg mixture, whisking constantly.

Divide the mixture between 6 ramekins and place in a bain marie. Bake in a cool oven, 140°C, for 20 to 25 minutes. The brûlée should still wobble slightly in the centre. Remove from the bain-marie and chill.

To serve

Cover the surfa grill.

Ingredients

8 egg yolks
50g caster sugar
450ml double cream
150ml Baileys liqueur
sugar to glaze

030
THE BELL AT SKENFRITH

Skenfrith, Monmouthshire NP7 8UH

01600 750 235
www.skenfrith.co.uk

The Bell is a Restaurant with Rooms that is perfectly situated on the banks of the River Monnow in the tiny village of Skenfrith, Monmouthshire. Surrounded by rolling countryside and numerous Marches castles and churches, this former 17th century Welsh coaching inn was carefully and thoughtfully restored in 2001 by William and Janet Hutchings.

Picture the scene: flagstone floors, oak beams and antique furniture, log fires when needed, comfy sofas and chairs all combine to create an easy and relaxing atmosphere. Upstairs are eleven individually decorated, en-suite bedrooms with crisp, white linens, fluffy towels and traditional Welsh wool blankets.

Downstairs, The Bell's Long Bar offers a range of local beer, cider and perry, early-landed cognacs and, most importantly, William's beloved wine list which has won numerous awards for its breadth and reasonable price tags.

The Bell's restaurant adjoins the bar; fresh flowers on the tables, starched linen napkins and candles in the evening all combine to create an amiable atmosphere. Outside is a pretty garden terrace for al fresco dining and a private dining room is the perfect venue for special events, weddings and parties.

Food has always been a passion for Janet and William. As early advocates of Slow Food, The Bell's menus have always been seasonal, using food from known and trusted local suppliers, all of whom are proudly listed on the wall-mounted Suppliers Board and menus. Four years ago, the couple realised their dream of an organic kitchen garden which has added another dimension to Head Chef Rupert Taylor's menus. The latest addition to this has been the rearing of Saddleback Pigs for the menu, which has proved to be popular with locals, restaurant customers and visiting guests alike. Rupert and Head Gardener Michele Civil work closely together to plan and grow for the kitchen, ensuring that vegetables, fruits, herbs and salads are always fresh and plentiful.

the

at ske

In this picture, from left to right George Salaru, Rupert Taylor and Richard Hopkins

The two-rosette restaurant, under Head Chef Rupert Taylor, serves delicious, locally-produced food, much of it from The Bell's own organic kitchen garden. It's Welsh cuisine at its tastiest!

Visit Wales and The AA have awarded The Bell five stars and the restaurant two AA Rosettes. The Bell was voted Michelin Pub of the Year for Great Britain and Ireland in 2007 and recently won the AA Wine Award for Wales and the UK 2012

TRIO OF HERITAGE TOMATOES

SERVES 4-6

🍷 2005 Barbera d'Alba Conca del Grillo, Silvano
Bolmida, Piemonte, Italy

Ingredients

Tomato Sauce

250g tomatoes (freshly chopped)
25ml olive oil
100g onions (diced)
1 clove garlic (chopped)
pinch of salt
1 tbsp picked thyme
100ml white wine vinegar
10g caster sugar
20g tomato purée

Tomato and Basil Mousse

100g tomato sauce
1 leaf gelatine
100ml lightly whipped cream
2 basil leaves (finely chopped)

Tomato Consommé

500g Heritage tomatoes
2 basil leaves
200g icing sugar

Bloody Mary Sorbet

1 shallot
¼ cucumber
1 red pepper
8 Heritage tomatoes
2 tbsp lemon juice
2 tbsp tomato purée
2 tbsp glucose
40ml vodka
celery salt, Worcestershire sauce and
horseradish to taste

Method

For the tomato sauce

Heat the oil in a heavy-based saucepan then add the onions, garlic, salt and thyme. Sweat for 10 minutes and then add the white wine vinegar. Reduce the liquid until all of it has evaporated then add all of the other ingredients and cook for 30 minutes, stirring occasionally. Blend in a food processor until smooth.

For the tomato and basil mousse

Soak the gelatine in cold water then warm the tomato sauce and add the soaked gelatine to it. Cool slightly before folding in the basil and cream. Leave to set for 2 hours.

For the tomato consommé

Place all ingredients in a food processor and blitz. Drain through a muslin cloth overnight.

For the bloody mary sorbet

Place all ingredients in a blender and blend until smooth, then season with celery, salt, horseradish and Worcestershire sauce. Pass the mix through a fine sieve and freeze.

To serve

Slice fresh multi-coloured Heritage tomatoes, and dress with a little salt and olive oil. Then pour on the tomato sauce and arrange with a scoop of tomato mousse. Pour the consommé into a shot glass and arrange on plate. Just before serving, scoop a ball of Bloody Mary sorbet onto the plate and serve immediately.

PAN-FRIED FILLET OF BRILL, FENNEL CABBAGE, CITRUS DILL RISOTTO WITH ORANGE DRESSING

SERVES 4-6

🍷 *2010 Grüner Veltliner, Fass 4, Bernhard Ott, Donauland, Austria*

Ingredients

3kg brill (filleted)
16 Savoy cabbage leaves
1 fennel bulb
2 oranges (segmented)
1 bunch dill (chopped)
2tbsp fennel seeds
4 sticks celery (chopped)
1pt orange juice (fresh)
100g risotto rice
50g parmesan (grated)
1tbsp crème fraiche
knob of butter

Orange Dressing

400ml fresh orange juice
10g orange zest (grated)
30g caster sugar
300ml rapeseed oil
100ml water
50ml white wine vinegar

Janet and William Hutchings

Method

For the brill

Firstly, finely slice the cabbage and fennel then heat a heavy-based pan and add a knob of the butter and the fennel seed. Cook for 2 minutes to release the aromas, then add the fennel and cook for a further 5 minutes. Next, add the cabbage and cook for 5 minutes.

Heat the orange juice to a simmer, add the celery and cook until soft. Then heat a little oil in a pan and add the risotto rice, hot orange juice and celery, then cook until the rice is soft.

Finish the risotto with parmesan, crème fraiche, orange segments and chopped dill.

Heat a little oil in a frying pan and, when hot, add the fish and cook it until golden and crisp on the skin side. Then turn the fish over and remove the pan from the heat. Season with salt and lemon juice.

For the orange dressing

Reduce the juice and zest to 200ml before whisking in the oil and then the vinegar to emulsify it. Finally, add the sugar and water to the correct consistency.

To serve

Place the cabbage in a circular cutter on the plate and place a line of risotto along the plate, then slice the celery into small batons and criss-cross them over the risotto. Finally, place the fish on top of the cabbage and garnish with finely sliced fennel, fennel and orange powder, pea shoots and edible flowers.

TASTE OF THE GARDEN

SERVES 4-6

🍷 *2008 Savennières Clos des Perrières, Château Soucherie, Loire, France*

Ingredients

Lemon Verbena Panna Cotta

200ml milk
200ml double cream
40g caster sugar
10g verbena leaves
2 leaves gelatine

Sorrel Ice Cream

300ml milk
200ml double cream
6 egg yolks
60g caster sugar
10g milk powder
10g glucose
7g ascorbic acid
100g sorrel

Candied Beetroot

1 litre water
2 large beetroots or 6 small beetroots
200g caster sugar
200ml water (additional)

Method

For the lemon verbena panna cotta

Bring the milk, cream and sugar slowly to the boil and add the verbena leaves, then leave to infuse for 30 minutes.

Soak the gelatine in a little water then dissolve it over warm water and add it to the milk mix. Pass through a sieve, pour into dariole moulds and set aside in the fridge to set.

For the sorrel ice-cream

Bring the milk and cream slowly to the boil then separately whisk the egg yolks, sugar, glucose and milk powder until pale. Pour the milk/cream mix over the egg mixture and cook out to 82°C (over a pan of boiling water), stirring continuously.

Place the mixture in a blender and blitz along with the ascorbic acid and sorrel. When smooth, cool quickly over ice to stop discolouration, then churn or still freeze.

For the candied beetroot

Bring the 1 litre of water to the boil, add the beetroot and cook until soft. Once cooked, peel the beetroot while it is still hot.

Place the sugar and 200ml water in a pan and bring to a boil, then add the beetroot (if large, cut in quarters) and cook for 10 minutes. Then leave to cool.

To serve

Turn out the panna cotta and place onto a cold plate, then garnish with candied beetroots, wild strawberries, blackberries and blueberries. You can also use edible flowers (pansies and nasturtiams) and rosemary leaves. Take some of the beetroot syrup and drizzle it on the plate, then ball the ice cream and serve straight away.

Rupert Taylor and Michele Civil

040
THE CASTLE HOTEL

Kings Road, Carmathenshire SA20 0AP

01550 720 343
www.castle-hotel-llandovery.co.uk

For centuries, the Castle Hotel has been at the heart of the thriving Welsh market town of Llandovery, Carmarthenshire that is well known as an area for Welsh mystic culture, and steeped in a rich history. Llandovery is surrounded by three rivers, the Towy, the Bran, and the Gwydderig. Today it is a buzzing market town that still has a strong medieval feel.

We subscribe totally to the good old-fashioned concept of a Welsh country inn. A warm and friendly place to unwind, you'll find a proper, traditional bar with roaring fires to toast your toes on and plenty of comfy sofas in which to lose yourself with a good book or map. With the beautiful Carmarthen and Pembrokeshire coastlines nearby and the Brecon Beacons National Park next door, there are an unlimited number of places to explor).

Because we want you to relax completely our bedrooms promise comfort and style. Think airy and spacious with luxury beds to dream on, flat screen TVs, unfussy, stylish décor and you'll get the picture. The original rustic charm and character is still there, but we've added a few modern, fresh ideas.

Our number one priority, our big thing, has always been food, and specifically, really good, simple food. If you share this passion you'll love it here. Those tempting aromas wafting through the building are likely to be from our new Josper charcoal oven - a very clever indoor BBQ and chargrill.

Carmarthenshire is known as the 'Garden of Wales' so it's no surprise we are blessed with the best natural local larder imaginable

We guarantee you will enjoy some seriously good cooking by our talented kitchen team all served up with a big dollop of Welsh hospitality.

Welcome to the Castle – We look forward to meeting you.

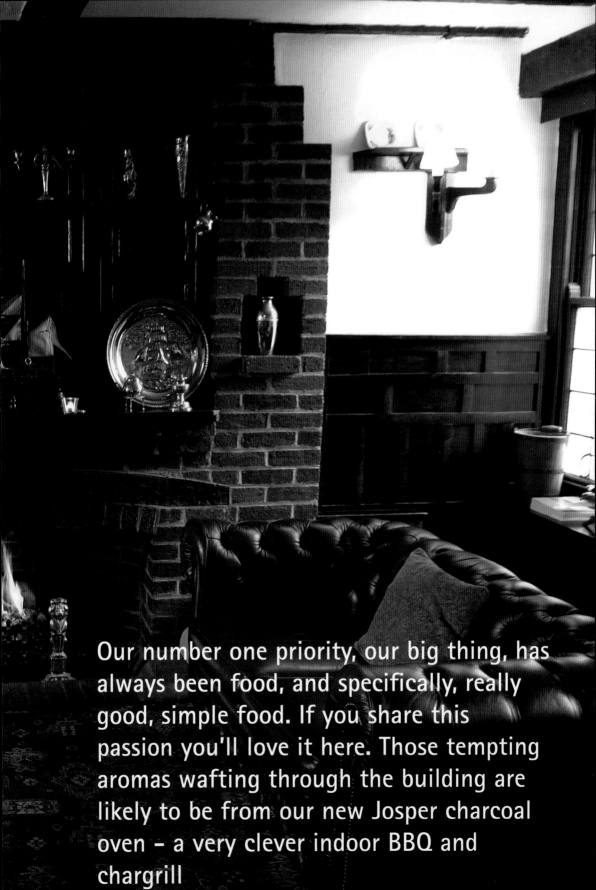

Our number one priority, our big thing, has always been food, and specifically, really good, simple food. If you share this passion you'll love it here. Those tempting aromas wafting through the building are likely to be from our new Josper charcoal oven – a very clever indoor BBQ and chargrill

GRIDDLED FRESH SQUID WITH WELSH CHORIZO, SAUTÉ POTATO, CHERRY TOMATO, WATERCRESS, AND ORANGE SAFFRON DRESSING

SERVES 4

 Sauvignon Blanc, The Frost Pocket 2010, Marlborough, New Zealand

Ingredients

2 x 150g squid (tubes cleaned and kept whole, with tentacles)
sea salt and freshly ground black pepper
chilli flakes
olive oil

1 bunch watercress
4 new potatoes (cooked)
100g chorizo (we use Trealy Farm, sliced into 5mm rings)
4 cherry tomatoes

½ pt orange juice
pinch saffron
75g sugar

Method

For the dressing

Put the orange juice, saffron, and sugar into a saucepan and gently bringing them to the boil without stirring. When the dressing coats the back of a spoon it is ready. This should take approximately 12- 15 minutes.

For the squid

Cut the tube along its length to create one large, flat piece. Lightly score the inside in a criss-cross pattern, but do not cut right through. Cut each squid into three equal pieces and thoroughly dry.

For the salad

Start by heating olive oil in a frying pan.

Take the chorizo and sauté it for about a minute to release the lovely saffron oil and then add the tomatoes until they blister a little. After approximately 2 minutes, remove the chorizo and tomato and keep warm until ready to serve. Use the oil from the chorizo pan and sauté the potatoes gently without them breaking until golden brown, then remove them from the pan and keep warm along with the chorizo and tomato.

To assemble

Place a griddle pan on a high heat.

Coat the squid and tentacles with oil and chilli flakes and season with salt and freshly ground black pepper. Place onto the hot griddle pan and turn them over after one minute, or when it curls, and take the squid off the heat.

In a bowl, put the watercress, the chorizo, tomato, potato and any chorizo juices together and mix them lightly. Then place the salad onto the middle of a plate.

To serve

Place the squid on the salad and dress the dish with the orange saffron dressing.

CHARCOAL GRILLED MIXED MEAT MEZZE BOARD

SERVES 2 AS A MAIN OR 4 AS A STARTER

Vallobera Crianza Rioja, Bodegas Vallobera, 2007

Ingredients

4 chicken thighs (boneless)
400g lamb shoulder (boneless)
4 metal skewers

Harissa Paste

4 large red chillies (chopped and deseeded)
6 cloves garlic (crushed)
25g fresh coriander
1 lemon (juice and zest only)
olive oil

Mini Burger

Small red onion (peeled and finely chopped)
sprig of fresh thyme leaves (chopped)
1 small egg
250g beef mince
oil for frying
salt and freshly ground black pepper

Broad Bean and Dill Hummus

400g broad beans (shelled)
4 tbsp olive oil
juice of ½ small lemon
few sprigs fresh dill

Griddled Flat Breads

½ tsp dried yeast
250ml warm water
500g plain or wholemeal flour or a mix of both
60ml extra virgin olive oil
sea salt, for sprinkling

Tomato, Chilli, Red Onion Salad

1 plum tomato (deseeded and chopped)
½ red onion (chopped)
dash of wine vinegar
dash of rapeseed oil
pinch of sugar and sea salt
small red chilli (finely chopped, seeds removed)
flat leaf parsley (chopped), fresh mint (chopped)
sugar to taste

Method

For the harissa

Use a food processor to pulse the ingredients together adding enough oil to give a paste like consistency.

Marinade the chicken and lamb in a small amount of the Harissa paste by massaging it gently into the meats. This will help to tenderise. Put the lamb onto the metal skewers, cover them and place in fridge until needed.

For the hummus

To make the broad bean hummus, cook the beans in boiling, lightly salted water until tender. This will take about 8-10 minutes, according to their size. Drain them, pop them out of their skins and blitz them to a thick purée in a food processor Then pour in the olive oil, with the blender still going, and also add the lemon juice and a grind of salt. Continue to blend until the mixture is smooth. Finely chop the dill and stir it in, then scrape the finished hummus into a dish and pour over a little olive oil.

For the burgers

Make the burgers by adding all the ingredients together and mixing them gently by hand. Be careful not to overwork the mix as it can make the burgers tough. Mould the burgers into small, individual patties. You should be able to make around six of them.

For the tomato salsa

Place the tomato, chopped onion and chilli into a non-reactive bowl, add a dash of rapeseed oil and wine vinegar and season with sea salt and sugar. Add the chopped parsley just before serving.

For the flat breads

Make the flat breads by dissolving the yeast in the warm water. Put the flour into a large mixing bowl and make a wide well in the middle. Gradually pour in the extra virgin olive oil and the water/yeast mixture and stir slowly with one hand, bringing the flour into the middle until it all comes together to form a dough. Using the ball of your hand, knead until your dough is elastic and smooth. Shape into a ball, cover with clingfilm and leave to rest for 1-2 hours in a warm, dry place. Divide the dough into six equal pieces and roll each one out to ½ cm (or less) thick. Sprinkle with sea salt and either bake in the oven on your preheated trays (drizzle the trays with extra virgin olive oil first) for 6-8 minutes, or until lightly golden, or lay them carefully on a hot griddle to grill for 2-3 minutes on each side until golden.

To serve

Grill (we use a charcoal grill) the prepared meat, until cooked to your liking and serve as in picture.

WARM RICH CHOCOLATE 'BLACK FOREST' FONDANT

SERVES 4

🍷 *Recioto Valpolicella Bertani, 2008*

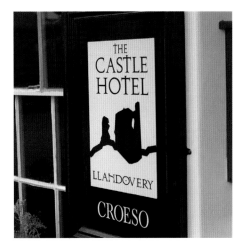

Ingredients

Chocolate Fondant

3 eggs
75g of caster sugar
45g of plain flour (sifted)
150g unsalted butter
150g dark chocolate pistoles

Chocolate Ganache

200ml double cream
100ml dark bitter chocolate 75%

Cherries in Red Wine

200g cherries (cut in half and stones removed)
50ml red wine
50g caster sugar
½ vanilla pod (seeds scraped out)

Method

For the chocolate fondant

Preheat the oven to 200°C, butter 4 x 6cm x 6cm size cake moulds and dust them with cocoa powder.

Whisk the eggs and sugar until pale and fluffy.

Over a pan of water melt the chocolate and the butter together.

Combine the egg mixture and the slightly cooled chocolate mixture and fold into the flour, mixing well.

Spoon the mixture about ½ way into the prepared moulds and place them on a baking tray in the centre of the preheated oven for 10 - 12 minutes.

For the chocolate ganache

In a small saucepan, bring the cream to the boil, remove the pan from the heat and add the chocolate, stir continuously until the chocolate has completely melted.

Pour the smooth chocolate ganache into a small container and leave to cool. Once cold, cover and refrigerate to set completely. Probably best to make this a day in advance to ensure that the ganache sets.

For the cherries in red wine

In a small saucepan bring the wine, vanilla seeds and sugar to the boil over a low heat. Reduce by half until syrupy.

Pour the hot syrup over the prepared cherries and leave to marinade. It's best to make this a day in advance.

To serve

Select a serving plate or plates, arrange the cakes on the plates and add a spoonful of the cherries on top, place a small quenelle of the chocolate ganache on top of the cherries and drizzle with a little of the red wine syrup.

050
THE CHECKERS

Broad Street, Montgomery, Powys SY15 6PN

01686 669 822
www.thecheckersmontgomery.co.u

M ontgomery, a former county town, enjoys a picturesque position with the Shropshire plains in the foreground and the rolling Welsh hills behind. This gentle and idyllic town hasn't always been a place of peace and tranquillity. Montgomery and its castle have been the scene of many fierce battles over the centuries as the English and Welsh fought for the borders.

Today Montgomery is a town proud of its heritage and sits firmly on the Welsh side of the border. A quiet and unobtrusive flow of visitors enjoy the steady pace and charm of this popular gateway to Wales.

Montgomery has some unusual links to France; indeed the town is named after Roger De Montgomery who was from Normandy in France.

Today the town has rekindled some of its French links, as Stéphane Borie, who hails from Agen in south west France, reopened The Checkers in early 2011. The former coaching inn on the town square today offers a relaxing bar and lounge, stylish restaurant and beautiful en-suite letting rooms.

Stéphane has a classic approach to cooking, with flavours and their combinations shining through in the menu and execution of dishes.

His kitchen apprenticeship began in France before moving to London in 1997. He went on to spend seven years with Michel Roux at The Waterside Inn Bray, the three Michelin-star training instilled excellence and dedication to his trade. The years of hard work were rewarded as The Checkers was awarded a Michelin star within its first year of trading.

Stéphane is joined at The Checkers by his long term partner Sarah Francis, who is also an accomplished chef, and Sarah's sister Kathryn, who manages front of house. The sisters are farmer's daughters from Shropshire and with Stéphane are known as 'The Frenchman and the farmer's daughters'. Stéphane's menu is complemented by an unpretentious and friendly service, a stylish and relaxing interior, and a beautiful town to enjoy.

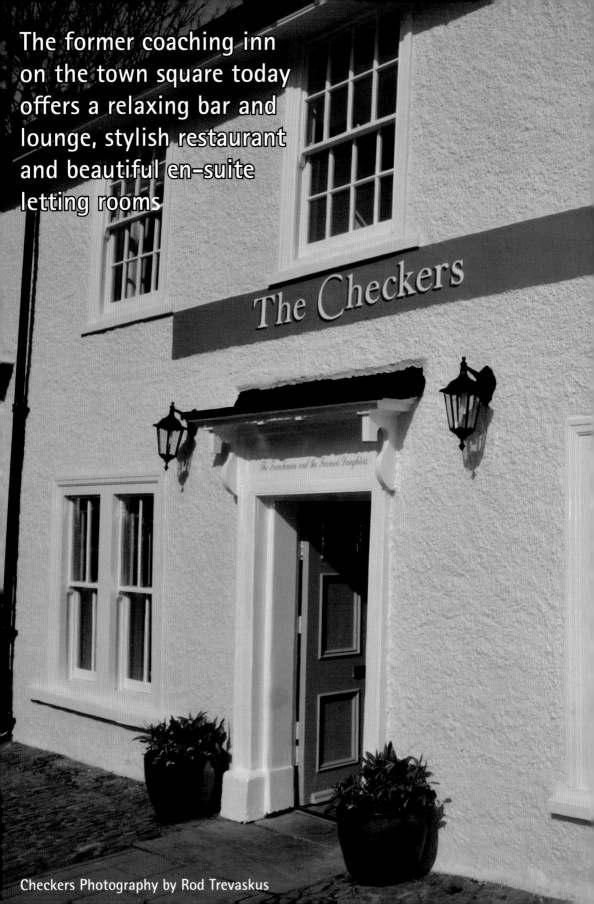

The former coaching inn on the town square today offers a relaxing bar and lounge, stylish restaurant and beautiful en-suite letting rooms

The Checkers

Checkers Photography by Rod Trevaskus

PITHIVERS OF PHEASANT AND FOIE GRAS WITH GRANNY SMITH AND WALNUT DRESSING

SERVES 6

Gewürztraminer, Pfaffenheim, Alsace, France 2010

Ingredients

Puff Pastry

one packet of all butter puff pastry

Pancakes

6 thin crepes (one per pithivers)

Pheasant Farce

100g pheasant breast
100g corn fed chicken breast
100g pork back fat
50g pheasant livers
100g double cream
1 egg yolk
a dash of port
a dash of brandy
10g tarragon, 10g chives
salt, pepper and cayenne pepper

Foie Gras Ballotine

(pre prepared foie gras terrine is fine to use if you do not wish to make your own)
200g raw foie gras des landes
3g salt
1g black pepper, 1g cayenne pepper
dash of Cognac, dash of white port

Sauce

500g of pheasant carcass
1 carrot, 1 celery stick, 2 shallots
1litre game stock
500ml veal stock
2 cloves of garlic
3 sprigs of thyme

Garnish

35 walnuts
250ml milk
2 granny smith apples (peeled and diced into 1cm square cubes and coated in olive oil and chives)

Method

For the farce

Dice all the meat and fat and place in a bowl with a dash of port and brandy. Cover and marinate in the fridge for twenty four hours. Pass the mix through a mincer and fold in the egg yolk, herbs and seasoning with a spatula. Now slowly add the double cream. Fry a little of the mixture to test the seasoning and correct as necessary. Finally, cover with clingfilm and place in the fridge

For the ballotine

Vacuum pack 200g of foie gras des landes and leave in the bag for one hour in cold water (this will make it softer and easier to de-nerve). Once soft, open the bag and de-nerve with some tweezers. Put three layers of clingfilm onto a smooth surface and place the prepared foie gras onto the clingfilm. Season with salt, pepper, cayenne and add the port and cognac. Roll into a sausage, with about 3cms in diameter and cook at 58°C in a pan of simmering water for eight minutes. Refresh in cold water and place in the fridge

For the walnuts

Boil the walnuts in 250ml of milk and leave for 5 minutes. Peel the outer layer of skin with a sharp knife. Fry the peeled walnuts in 'beurre noisette' (brown butter) until golden brown. Reserve.

For the sauce

Roast the carcass until golden brown. Add the vegetables and colour. Add the wine and reduce by half. Add the stock and boil. Cook for an hour. Pass through a sieve and reduce. Add garlic and thyme and infuse in the sauce for ten minutes. Pass through a muslin cloth and reserve

To assemble

Pre heat the oven to 220°C. Roll out the puff pastry until 2mm thick and cut 6 circles with a 10cm cutter and a further 6 with a 2cm cutter. Take the pancakes and cut 6 circles with an 8cm cutter and 6 with a 4 cm cutter. Egg wash the largest pastry disc and place the largest pancake disk in the centre.

Flour the inside of 6 small cups and place the large pastry and pancake disks in the centre of the cup and half fill with farce.

Cut the foie gras into 1cm discs and place on top of the farce. Fill the remainder of the cup with farce, finishing with the small pancake disk and finally the smallest pastry disk. Seal pastry edges together. Remove from the moulds and place in the fridge for 10 minutes.

Glaze with egg wash and score as illustrated with a sharp knife. Bake for 14 minutes. Serve with dressed green leaves, walnuts, granny smith apple a drizzle of sauce.

CRISPY MARCHES PORK BELLY WITH BAKED MASHED POTATO, CARAMELISED PEAR & BRAISING JUS

SERVES 6

 Régnié, Château Chassantour, M. Perroud, Beaujolais, France

Ingredients

Pork Belly

½ side of pork belly (bones removed and retained)
100g coarse salt

Braising Liquor

3 litres chicken stock
1 litre veal stock
2 carrots
4 shallots
1 celery stick
500ml white wine

Caramelised Pears

1 cinnamon stick
10 conference pears
2 litres water
500g sugar
1 lemon

Creamed Potato

12 large désirée potatoes
200ml double cream
100g butter

Method

Braising the pork belly

Score the skin on the pork belly and cut into 5 x 8 cm pieces. Sprinkle liberally with coarse salt and put in the fridge for 90 minutes.

Chop up the reserved bones and colour in a frying pan. Add the vegetables and lightly colour. Add the white wine and reduce by half. Transfer to a large pan and add the chicken and veal stock, cover and simmer.

Wash the salt off the pork belly and add to the pan of stock, cover and simmer for two hours. Leave the pork belly to cool in the stock.

For the braising jus

Take the cooled braising liquor and pass through a conical sieve. Now reduce the stock to a light jus consistency and reserve.

For the creamed potato

Bake 12 large désirée for 1½ hours at 220°C. Scoop out the centre of the potato and mash while very hot. In a pan warm the cream and add to the potato followed by the butter. Season with salt and white pepper.

For the caramelised pears

Put all of the ingredients except the pears in a pan and bring to the boil. Peel and core the pears and put in the pan - poached gently until tender. Blitz 3 of the pears in a blender until very smooth and keep aside.

To serve

Place the pork belly squares in a non-stick pan skin side down and roast in a pan for 15 minutes at 200°C. Slice the remaining whole poached pears into wedges, and put in a separate pan and roast at the same time as the pork belly. Remove the pork belly and pears from the oven and serve with the baked mashed potato, pear purée and roasted pears and braising jus.

AGEN PRUNE SOUFFLÉ WITH VANILLA ICE CREAM & CARAMEL SAUCE

SERVES 6

🍷 *Moscato d'Asti Vigna Senza Nome, Giacomo Bologna, Italy*

Ingredients

Prune Purée
250g pitted Agen prune
250ml strong tea

Crème Pâtissière
250g milk
250g prune pulp
100g sugar,
25g flour
5 egg yolks
125ml Armagnac

Soufflé
160g above crème patissiere
160g egg whites
30g sugar

Prune Garnish
28 pitted prunes, Armagnac to cover

Ice Cream
2 vanilla pods
600m double cream
8 egg yolks
225g sugar

Caramel Sauce
75m sugar
50ml water
375ml double cream

Method

For the prune purée
Soak 250g prunes in strong tea for two hours. Then blitz in a tall blender to make a pulp and pass through a conical sieve.

For the crème pâtissière
Boil the milk. In a separate pan, whisk the egg yolks and sugar until pale and add the flour. Pour the milk over the mixture and cook for one minute, stirring continuously. Take off the heat and add the prune purèe and Armagnac to taste.

For the caramel sauce
In a heavy based pan bring the sugar and water to the boil. Heat without stirring until the sugar turns a caramel colour. Turn off the heat and stir in the cream and pass through a fine sieve and reserve.

For the ice cream
Whisk the cream to a ribbon consistency and set aside in the fridge. Put the sugar in a pan and cook to 121°C, when it reaches 115°C start to beat the egg yolks. Pour the sugar over the egg yolks and beat until cool. Fold the cream into the egg yolks and freeze immediately.

Preparing the moulds
Take 6 ramekins and butter thoroughly. Place in the fridge for 10 minutes and rebutter a second time and then coat with sugar.

Cooking the soufflé
Pre heat the oven to 220°C then warm 160g of the crème pâtissière in a pan.

In a separate bowl, whisk 160g of egg whites and add 30g sugar, then whisk to form soft peaks. Thoroughly whisk 1/3 of the meringue into the warm pâtissière. Now add the remaining whites and gently fold in – do not over work. Half fill the ramekins with the mix.

Dice 10 of the reserved prunes and put on top of the soufflé mix and cover with the remaining mix. Smooth the top and the edge of the ramekin with a palate knife. Place in the oven and cook for 4 minutes on one side and 3 minutes on the other.

To serve
Remove from the oven, dust with icing sugar, garnish with a whole prune and serve with warm caramel sauce and ice cream immediately.

060
THE CROWN AT CELTIC MANOR

The Celtic Manor Resort, Coldra Woods, Newport, South Wales NP18 1HQ

01633 410 262
www.crown.celtic-manor.com

A s the host venue of The 2010 Ryder Cup, the world-renowned Celtic Manor Resort offers luxury on a grand scale. It encompasses a wealth of exceptional facilities set amongst 1,400 acres of panoramic parkland in the beautiful Usk Valley, South Wales.

The Crown at Celtic Manor is the five star resort's flagship fine dining venue; the product of an exciting partnership between The Celtic Manor Resort and Michelin starred restaurant, The Crown at Whitebrook. Newport-born James Sommerin, who has won and retains a Michelin Star at The Crown at Whitebrook, is the executive chef at both restaurants, while Tim McDougall delivers his vision as the head chef of The Crown at Celtic Manor.

Opening in April 2008 and quickly gaining recognition for its culinary excellence, including a listing in The Good Food Guide 2009, The Crown at Celtic Manor was awarded three AA Rosettes within its first year of operation, and was one of only seventeen new recipients of the prestigious award in 2009, of which only three were awarded outside London.

As well as an à la carte menu, The Crown also offers an express one-hour lunch menu, which is ideal for business diners, and an exciting six course tasting menu each evening. Each dish is intricately created with a strong emphasis on seasonality and the use of locally-sourced ingredients, producing fresh, intense and punchy flavours for an unforgettable culinary experience.

An atmospheric private lounge and bar provides the perfect place to relax before dining, where guests can linger over the menu and enjoy a pre-dinner drink with complimentary canapés. For group dining with a unique twist, the Crown's private Chef's Table offers diners a unique insight into the art and intensity of a dynamic fine-dining kitchen.

The Crown at Celtic Manor was awarded three AA Rosettes within its first year of operation and was one of only seventeen new recipients of the prestigious award in 2009, of which only three were awarded outside London

SEARED SCALLOPS, LETTUCE VELOUTÉ AND SPICED SWEETBREADS

SERVES 4

🍷 *MandraRossa Fiano di Sicilia, Italy 2010*

Ingredients

8 large scallops
200g veal sweetbreads

Lettuce Velouté

3 heads round lettuce
1 small onion
1 medium floury potato
150g butter
500ml milk
crème fraîche
salt and pepper

Curry Spice for Sweetbreads

1 pinch cardamom seeds
1 dsp coriander
2 pinches ground cinnamon
1 tsp onion seeds
1 dsp garam masala
2 pinches dry ginger
1 tbsp curry powder
large sprig thyme
bay leaf

Method

For the lettuce velouté

Pick the outer, dark-green leaves from the lettuce and set them to one side. Chop up the hearts and stalks, slice the onion and dice the potato. Melt the butter in a saucepan and sweat the vegetables, without colouring them, for around 10 minutes. Add the milk and simmer until the potato is cooked. Add the lettuce leaves and remove the pan from the heat. Leave to stand for two minutes and then liquidise the assorted lettuce parts and vegetables. Adjust the seasoning and pass through a fine sieve, then chill quickly to retain colour, ideally in a bowl over some ice.

For the sweetbread curry spice

Place all of the ingredients together on a tray and leave them to dry until the thyme leaves are crispy and fall away from the stalk. Then break them up in a spice grinder or pestle and mortar and scrape through a sieve.

For the sweetbreads and scallops

Blanch the sweetbreads ahead of time in salt water with a dash of vinegar. Remove them from the water when they begin to firm up. Remove any membranes, then cut the sweetbreads into scallop-sized pieces and coat with some of the spice mix and a little vegetable oil.

To finish

Fry the scallops and sweetbreads together in a non-stick pan with a little oil. When they are golden brown, add a knob of butter and squeeze in some lemon juice. Serve with the chilled lettuce velouté.

To serve

At the restaurant we like to serve this dish with pea shoots, dandelion leaves, and a lemon vinaigrette with summer truffle.

ROAST SKATE WING, BROCCOLI PURÉE, ORANGE AND CORIANDER GEL

SERVES 6

Heller Estate Chenin Blanc, Carmel Valley, California 2007

Ingredients

6 x 150g small skate wings
lemon juice
knob of butter

Broccoli Purée

600g broccoli
300ml milk (approx)
100g butter
olive oil

Orange and Coriander Gel

300ml orange juice
600ml chicken stock
20g coriander seeds
1 bunch fresh coriander
3g gellan gum type F

Method

For the broccoli purée

Break the broccoli down into small pieces, reserving a few florets for the garnish, then sweat them briefly in the butter and oil. Now add the milk until it just covers the top of the broccoli and season as desired. Boil until soft and liquidise to a smooth purée. Drop the reserved florets into boiling, salted water for about five minutes or until just soft and serve warm, dressed in melted butter or olive oil.

For the orange and coriander gel

Place the orange juice and coriander seeds into a pan and reduce by about two thirds then add the chicken stock and further reduce by about one third. Add the fresh coriander and leave to infuse into the liquid for five minutes. Pass the mixture through a sieve and measure 400ml of the remaining stock, then return it to a small pan and bring almost to the boil. Whisk in the gellan powder and continue to whisk on a low heat for one minute, then pour into a bowl over ice and whisk until it sets and becomes a gel. If it becomes lumpy or grainy, simply pulse in a food processor and pass it through a fine sieve.

For the fish

Fry one side of the skate in light olive oil in a non-stick pan until golden brown. Turn the fish over and then add a knob of butter and a squeeze of lemon juice. Baste the fish until it is warm in the centre.

To serve

Arrange on the plate as per the picture.

WHITE CHOCOLATE MOUSSE, RASPBERRY JUS, SABLÉ BISCUIT

SERVES 8

🍷 *Ernst Triebaumer Eiswein, Ruster, Austria 2008*

Ingredients

White Chocolate Mousse

1 egg
2 egg yolks
100g sugar
300g white cooking chocolate
200ml double cream

Raspberry Jus

200g fresh raspberries
65g caster sugar

Sablé Biscuit

110g butter
50g sugar
half vanilla pod
pinch of salt
160g plain flour

Method

For the white chocolate mousse

Whisk the egg and egg yolks with an electric whisk. Separately, add a splash of water to the sugar and boil it until it reaches 120°C, then add this to the egg whilst whisking continually. Whisk the mixture until it has cooled to room temperature. Next, melt the chocolate and mix in. Whip the cream to soft peaks and fold it together with the chocolate, egg and sugar mixture. Leave to chill and set before serving.

For the raspberry jus

Place the ingredients into a glass or metal bowl and place over a pan of simmering water for one hour, then pass through a clean cloth or coffee filter to obtain a clear liquid.

For the sablé

Cream the butter and sugar with the seeds from the vanilla pod until white and very soft. The easiest way to do this is in an electric mixer with a paddle attachment. Then add the rest of the ingredients and mix until smooth. Pipe the mixture into shaped moulds and bake at 170°C for about nine minutes, or until golden brown. Allow to cool before serving.

To serve

Arrange on the plate as per the picture.

070
THE CROWN AT WHITEBROOK

Whitebrook, near Monmouth, Monmouthshire, NP25 4TX

01600 860 254
www.crownatwhitebrook.co.uk

The Crown at Whitebrook, nestling in the heart of the Wye Valley Area of Outstanding Natural Beauty, near Monmouth, is a shining and illustrious beacon of gastronomy in Wales. Supremely talented Welsh born James Sommerin, celebrated for his consummate ability to deconstruct and re-interpret classic dishes, is the Executive Head Chef at Michelin-starred The Crown at Whitebrook and also its sister restaurant, the three AA Rosette Awarded Crown at Celtic Manor Resort, venue of the 2010 Ryder Cup.

The Crown at Whitebrook established in 1971, gained its first Michelin star in 2007 and it has retained this ever since. Set in a C17th drover's inn in three acres of tranquil landscaped Monmouthshire gardens and surrounded by forest views, The Crown is one of just four restaurants in Wales to hold a Michelin star. Offering a modern British menu with classical French disciplines, The Crown, which also holds three AA Rosettes, was listed 28th in The Good Food Guide's Top 50 restaurants in the UK 2012 and named the best in Wales, 30th in the Guide's Top 60 in 2011 and was 36th the year before in the Top 50. Throughout the restaurant has maintained its impressive cooking score of 7/10.

Every ingredient is meticulously selected and much thought is given, as to how the combination of ingredients will look on the plate and how the flavours will taste on the palate. Sourcing as much fresh and local produce whenever and wherever possible is key to The Crown's cooking.

Almost everything used in the kitchen is sourced locally from selected Monmouthshire farms while foraged leaves and mushrooms come from nearby woods and meadows.

The restaurant's 250 excellent wines on its award winning list are each categorised by grape variety.

Smart, contemporary and modern The Crown at Whitebrook, named True Taste of Wales Restaurant of the Year in 2010, has comfortable, deep leather arm chairs and sofas with original artwork hanging on the walls in the lounge. Upstairs there are eight luxurious bedrooms with en-suite modern bathrooms, based on The Crown's Welsh heritage, each boasts a unique character, individually styled and named after a famous Welsh personality.

And all this is topped off with simply flawless service.

Set in a C17th drover's inn in three acres of tranquil and beautifully landscaped Monmouthshire gardens and surrounded by forest views, The Crown is one of just four restaurants in Wales to hold a Michelin star

MACKEREL, WHITE CHOCOLATE, HORSERADISH, BEETROOT

SERVES 6

Bourgogne Aligote, 2006, Domaine Ramonet, Burgundy, France

Ingredients

Mackerel Fillets

6 x 80g mackerel fillets (with skin on)
1 tbsp olive oil

Crumb Mixture

40g butter
35g milk powder
40g plain flour
15g cornflour
20g caster sugar
sea salt

White Chocolate

75g fresh horseradish
100g white chocolate
35g milk powder

Mackerel Tartare

4 mackerel fillets (skinned)
juice of ½ lemon
50ml olive oil
2 shallots
salt
pepper

Beetroot Reduction

100ml beetroot juice
beetroot
bay leaf
150ml balsamic vinegar
45g caster sugar
225ml apple juice

To Plate

edible flowers to garnish
olive oil

Method

Start by dicing the beetroot into 1cm pieces then bring the beetroot juice, balsamic vinegar, bay leaf, caster sugar and apple juice to the boil, adding the diced beetroot after the mixture starts boiling. Place this in a covered container and leave to pickle in the refrigerator for approximately 24 hours.

After the beetroot is done pickling, take a third of the pickling liquid and reduce it by half in a saucepan. Reserve the reduction in the fridge, aside from the rest of the mixture.

Next, preheat the oven to 120°C/Gas mark 1, melt the butter and mix it with the milk powder, plain flour, cornflour, caster sugar and a pinch of sea salt. Place on a baking sheet and bake for 10 minutes, then leave to cool.

Finely grate the fresh horseradish and mix with the white chocolate and milk powder in a saucepan until the chocolate has melted.

Fold in the crumb mixture and place on a baking tray in the fridge to cool.

For the mackerel tartare

Finely chop the mackerel fillets and mix with the olive oil, the lemon juice, the finely chopped shallots and a pinch of salt and pepper. Leave for 5 minutes before serving.

In a hot pan, sear the mackerel, skin-side down, in a little olive oil for between 30 seconds to a minute, then turn and repeat. The mackerel should be slightly undercooked and translucent in the centre.

To serve

Quenelle the mackerel tartare. Sweep the beetroot reduction onto each plate and place a mackerel fillet on top. Place the tartare on the side of the plate, scattering over the pickled beetroot chunks, the biscuit crumb, some wildflowers and a drizzle of olive oil.

PORK WITH DATES AND FIVE SPICE

SERVES 6

Pinot Noir, Au Bon Climat, 2009, Santa Barbara Valley, California, USA

Ingredients

Pig's Head and Tails

1 onion (roughly chopped)
1 leek (roughly chopped)
2 carrots (roughly chopped)
6 leaves of Savoy cabbage
1 tbsp olive oil
½ pig's head
2 pigs' tails
200ml red wine
sprig of fresh thyme
1 tbsp sherry vinegar
100g plain flour
2 eggs
100g panko breadcrumbs

Pork Tenderloins

2 x 200g pork tenderloins
2 tbsp olive oil

Date Puree

250g Medjool dates (stones removed, simmer until soft and blitz)

Pan-fried vegetables

2 butternut squashes (only need tops)
1 head of broccoli
6 baby leeks
50g butter
1 tbsp five spice
salt and pepper

Pork Belly

1 onion
1 leek
2 carrots
1 tbsp olive oil
400g pork belly (with skin on)
200ml red wine
sprig of fresh thyme

Method

For the pig's head and tails

Brown the onion, leek and carrots in the olive oil at a high heat, add the pig's head and pig's tails, colour slightly. Deglaze with wine. Add the thyme, cover with water. Cover with foil and simmer for 3 hours.

For the pork belly

In a second pot, use the same method for the pork belly and add cubed butternut squash.

Remove the pork belly from the liquid and press between 2 trays. Set it in the refrigerator overnight, using a heavy weight to keep the pork belly pressed flat.

Take the pig's head and tails out of the water. When cool enough, pick out the cheek and any meaty bits from the pig's head in small pieces, discarding all bones and any large pieces of fat or skin. Mix the meat from the pig's head in a bowl with the sherry vinegar. Cut down the length of the tails and carefully pull out the bones. Roll them into sausage-shaped cylinders, wrapping them tightly in clingfilm twisted at the ends, and leave them in the refrigerator to set for about an hour. Cut the pork belly into rectangular pieces 2cm wide and set aside.

For the vegetables

Cut the broccoli into florets. Blanch for 2 minutes with the leeks and squash, refresh in ice water. Melt the butter, add the five spice, squash, leeks and broccoli and cook over a moderate heat for 4-5 minutes until tender. Season with salt and pepper.

Cut the pork tails into 2cm pieces. Place the flour, eggs and breadcrumbs onto separate plates. Roll the tail in the flour, then the eggs, the breadcrumbs, the egg and the breadcrumbs again, coating lightly each time. Weigh the head meat into 30g pieces and pack into balls.

Cut out the ribs of the Savoy cabbage and blanch in boiling water for 30 seconds, refreshing in ice water. Wrap each ball of head meat in a leaf of cabbage. Wrap in clingfilm then put the head meat parcels into simmering water to reheat before serving. Sear each rectangle of belly pork for 1 minute on each side.

Deep-fry the pig's tail in a deep-fat fryer at 190°C for 3 minutes, set aside. Trim the pork loin of their sinews and warm in a roasting pan at 240°C for 2 minutes along with the belly pork.

To serve

Sweep a portion of the date purée along each plate, top with a portion of the pig's tail, pork belly, loin, cabbage-wrapped meat and vegetables.

LEMON CURD WITH BLACKCURRANT SORBET, OATMEAL, AND MINT GLASS

SERVES 6

La Beryl Blanc, 2010, Fairview Estate, Paarl, South Africa

Ingredients

Lemon Curd

5 eggs
55g caster sugar
90ml lemon juice
100g butter

Oatmeal

170g oats
55g plain flour
30g caster sugar
½ tsp salt
¼ tsp sodium bicarbonate
110g butter

Blackcurrant Sorbet

125ml water
125g caster sugar
20g glucose
500ml blackcurrant purée

Mint Glass

50ml liquid glucose
50g isomalt
100g fondant icing
20 fresh mint leaves plus extra to garnish

Italian Meringue

200g caster sugar
80ml water
20g glucose
3 eggs

Method

Preheat the oven to 180°C/Gas mark 4. To make the lemon curd, separate 3 of the eggs and combine 3 egg yolks with 2 whole eggs and the sugar and lemon juice.

Then whisk this mixture over a bain-marie until thick. Once thick, finish with the butter, whisking until fully incorporated.

For the oatmeal

Mix all the dry ingredients together then melt the butter, pour it into the dry mixture and mix well.

Place the oatmeal in an airtight container and bake it in the oven for 9 minutes when required.

For the sorbet

Prepare a stock syrup by boiling the water along with an equal amount of sugar and the glucose. As soon as the mixture boils, remove from the heat and stir. This can be done in advance and refrigerated until it is needed.

Boil the blackcurrant purée with 250ml of the stock syrup.

After the mixture has been brought to a boil, remove it from the heat, allow it to cool and place in an ice cream machine until frozen. Remove when finished and place in freezer.

For the mint glass

Place all the ingredients in a pan except the mint. Bring to 140°C then pour onto a baking sheet and leave to cool.

As the glass is cooling, place the mint leaves on the top. Allow to cool completely until solidified. Once cool, place into a blender and blend to a fine powder, then place back onto a baking sheet.

Bake in the oven at 200°C, checking regularly until the sugar melts and forms a clear sheet. Allow to cool at room temperature.

To make the meringue, boil the sugar, water and glucose to 120°C. Then separate the eggs and whisk the egg whites to soft peaks. Pour the hot sugar mixture slowly onto the egg whites and keep whisking until cool.

To serve

Place some oatmeal crumbs in the bottom of 6 small bowls and pipe lemon curd over the top. Include a small sprinkling of oatmeal, a small scoop of sorbet, a shard of mint glass and a swipe of the Italian meringue, toasted with a blowtorch, in each bowl. Garnish with a sprig of mint.

080
THE FELIN FACH GRIFFIN

Felin Fach, Brecon LD3 0UB

01874 620 111
www.felinfachgriffin.co.uk

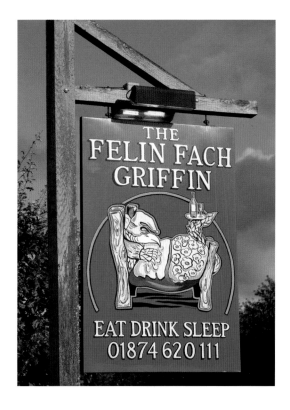

Soda bread baked this morning. Muddy carrots picked in the kitchen garden. The fugitive smell of a rib-eye seared on the grill. Crisp linen, the most comfortable beds and a steaming bath. Village residents dropping in for a drink on their way home. Tomos Watkin OSB by the fire. These are just some of the things that go to make The Felin Fach Griffin a special place.

Brought back to life in 2000, it has consistently been recognised as one of the best of that new breed of dining pubs that has taken the starch out of eating out in Britain.

Head Chef, Ross Bruce, is rooted in the Welsh countryside, brought up, like owners Charles and Edmund Inkin, in neighbouring Monmouthshire. He feels strongly about sourcing his ingredients properly and about bringing a slower pace of life to this corner of the Welsh Mountains.

Julie Bell hosts with a huge dollop of Ulster energy and runs a team nearly all brought up in the lee of the Brecon Beacons. Each is tasked with ensuring that every guest leaves The Griffin with their belief restored in the value of the simple things in life done well.

The Griffin's seven bedrooms become a logical end of the line for many of its guests' journey, the inclusive Sleepover rates much in demand. EATDRINKSLEEP is after all the name of the Inkin brothers' company, through which they own sister Inns in Cornwall, The Gurnard's Head near St. Ives and The Old Coastguard in Mousehole.

Brought back to life in 2000, it has consistently been recognised as one of the best of that new breed of dining pubs that has taken the starch out of eating out in Britain

PORK AND PISTACHIO RILLETTES WITH DAILY BREAD

SERVES 4

🍷 *Jurançon Sec, Domaine Montesquiou*

Ingredients

Pork Belly Rillette

600g belly pork
1 litre of duck fat
200g sea salt
1 small bunch of thyme
2 bulbs of garlic
200g unsalted pistachios (toasted)

Daily Bread

250g strong white flour
180g water
2g instant yeast
5g sea salt

Method

For the pork belly

Remove any bones or cartilage from the meat and lay it out in a deep tray that fits in the fridge. Sprinkle the flesh side liberally with the salt. Wrap tightly and leave overnight. The following morning remove the pork from the fridge and dispose of the salt crust. Leave the meat in the tray under flowing cold water for about 3 minutes or until the water tastes fresh and unsalted.

Drain the water away and pat the pork belly dry with a paper towel. Lay the meat in a tin and cover with duck fat. You may need more or less than 1 litre, it depends on the size of your tin but the pork should be entirely covered by about 2cms. Cover with foil and bake in an oven set to 150°C for about 5 hours. The end result should be slightly caramelised fat and skin and meat that tries to fall apart when you touch it.

For the rillette

Allow to cool slightly then carefully remove the meat and allow it to drain off any excess fat. While it is still warm shred half of the meat with your fingers and pick the other half into slightly bigger chunks. Mix the meat together carefully in a bowl. Squeeze the remaining fat from the meat over the mixture.

I know this seems frighteningly unhealthy but it is essential for taste and it will aid the pots to set.

Roughly chop the pistachios and add two thirds of them to the mix. Carefully mix everything together, keeping the textures and check the seasoning. Set into little jam jars or kilners and press them down so that the tops are level. Pour on half a centimetre of duck fat, sprinkle with the remaining pistachios and leave to set in the fridge until cold.

For the daily bread

Mix the flour with the water to a rough dough. Cover and leave to stand for ten minutes. Add the yeast and salt and mix again, knead for 8 minutes to a smooth, silky stretchy dough. Transfer the dough to an oiled tub and leave to proof to one and a half times its size. Remove the dough and turn out onto a very lightly floured surface. With your hands press it out into a rectangle and fold it like a letter. Flip it over and put back into the tub you first proofed it in. Allow the dough to rise again to one times its original size. Turn it back out and shape into either a long baguette or two smaller ones, place on a tray and cover tightly. Proof the loaves to one and a half their original size, slash the tops with a sharp knife and bake in an oven set to 210°C for about 15 minutes or until they are the colour of dark caramel.

To serve

Serve the rillettes cold with warm bread and a handful of pickles.

POTATO GNOCCHI WITH POT ROASTED CAULIFLOWER, MUSCAT GRAPES AND TICKLEMORE CHEESE

SERVES 4

 *Grünear Veltliner, Markus Huber*

Ingredients

Potato Gnocchi

750g red Duke of York potatoes
190g plain flour
2 egg yolks
nutmeg
salt and white pepper

Roasted Cauliflower

1 head of cauliflower (leaves removed and cut into florets)
80g honey
100g butter
thyme leaves
salt and pepper

2 shallots (shredded)
1 tsp garlic purée
about 300g Muscat grapes (washed, stalks removed)
250g Ticklemore cheese
1 bunch mizuna salad leaves (washed)

Method

For the potato gnocchi

Wash the skins of the potatoes well and place in cold salted water. Bring to boil and simmer for about 15 minutes or until the potatoes can be pierced but are still very firm. Do not cool the potatoes at any point, for the gnocchi to work the dough needs to be kept as hot as possible. Peel the potatoes. Put the peeled potatoes through a ricer and mix with sieved the flour, nutmeg and seasoning until it forms a rough dough. Add the egg yolks and mix a little more. Turn out onto a lightly floured surface and knead by hand, working quickly to keep the temperature in the dough until you have a smooth ball.

Remove a piece of dough (about the size of an apple) and wrap the rest in a cloth to keep warm. Roll the dough into a long cylinder with a diameter of about one centimetre. Cut through the cylinder at 2 centimetre intervals, forming the start of the gnocchi. With a butter knife in one hand and a fork in the other, push each gnocchi with the knife towards the back of the fork and with a little flick of the wrist roll it up the back. This will crimp the gnocchi and give it a little structure. When you have crimped one cylinder, place on a lightly floured tray and set aside. Repeat the process until all the gnocchi are crimped. Cook in rapidly boiling salted water. They will only take a few minutes and you will know when they are cooked as they will begin to float. Transfer to ice-cold water, drain thoroughly and toss in a little olive oil. Set Aside.

For the cauliflower

Try to keep all the florets roughly the size of a golf ball. Heat a pan large enough to house all the cauliflower in one layer, add plenty of oil. Add the cauliflower so that all the stalks are pointing out of the pan and keep on a moderately high heat. You should be able to hear it cooking but not so hot that it smokes. Season. When the florets are a deep golden brown add the butter and cook for another five minutes. Add the honey and increase the heat. All the juices will ooze from the cauliflower and will be emulsified with the honey and butter. Continue cooking until the stalks are tender, stir in the thyme leaves and remove from the heat. Set aside in the juice.

To serve

Heat a large pan or non-stick roasting tray and add a little oil to fry the shallots then add the gnocchi and cook until evenly browned. Add the grapes and cook until slightly blistered, then stir in the cauliflower and half of the juice. Adding it all may make the dish too sweet. Season well and stir in the garlic purée. Transfer to a warm serving dish and grate the Ticklemore cheese directly over the top. Toss the Mizuna in a little olive oil and lemon juice and scatter over the top.

GREEN APPLE MOUSSE WITH ALMOND COOKIE AND CALVADOS

SERVES 4

 Julian Temperley's 5yo Somerset Cider Brandy

Ingredients

Green Apple Mousse

2 egg whites
100g sugar
200g crème fraîche
100g double cream
150g green apple juice (freshly pressed)
1 healthy slug of apple brandy (ideally Somerset cider brandy)

Apple Crisps

1 or 2 large apples
50:50 stock syrup
lemon juice

Almond Cookie

25g unsalted butter
200g white chocolate pieces
200g toasted, flaked almonds
1 egg
85g soft brown sugar
45g flour
pinch of sea salt
¼ tsp of baking powder

Calvados Jelly

200g Calvados or cider brandy
100g apple juice
3 leaves of gelatine

Method

For the apple mousse

Put the sugar in a small pan with a few tablespoons of water and bring quickly to 117°C (soft ball stage). When the sugar is boiling put the whites into a stand up mixer fitted with a whisk attachment and switch it on to its lowest setting. When the sugar is up to temperature, quickly pour into the egg whites aiming for the deepest part so that none gets stuck to the side of the bowl and quickly turn up to full speed. Whisk until the meringue is shiny, brilliant white and cool.

Meanwhile you can whisk the crème fraîche, cream, apple juice and brandy until it forms soft peaks. Add a quarter of the crème fraîche mix onto the meringue and fold it carefully so as to slacken the mixtures to the same consistency. Now fold them together very carefully leaving as much air as possible in the mousse. Transfer into a sealed container into the fridge and chill for at least one hour to set.

For the almond cookie

Melt the butter with half the chocolate in a bain-marie. Beat the egg and sugar together then add the raw chocolate and almonds. Sieve the flour and baking powder together and add one third to the mix. Add a third of the chocolate butter mix and fold carefully. Continue to add the rest of the flour and chocolate butter mix one third at a time until all the ingredients are fully incorporated. Line a baking tray with buttered greaseproof paper and spread the mixture in one even layer. Bake in an oven preheated to 190°C for about 8 minutes or until dark golden brown. Remove from the oven and rest for five minutes before transferring to a cooling rack.

For the apple crisps

Bring syrup to the boil and allow to cool to room temperature. Add the juice of one lemon. Slice the apples as thinly as possible across the width so the core remains in the centre and place into the syrup. Layer the slices onto a baking tray lined with a non-stick mat and leave on a warm shelf to dry until crispy.

For the calvados jelly

Soak the gelatine in a little apple juice. Warm the calvados gently and stir in the soaked gelatine leaves before cooling to room temperature. Add the remaining apple juice and set in the fridge.

To serve

Snap the cookie into four pieces and place on top of a small spoonful of mousse. Spoon more mousse onto each piece of biscuit. Break some of the crisps and sprinkle with a few more toasted almonds. Add little pieces of the calvados jelly. Finish with a drizzle of honey, whole apple crisps and a sprinkling of wood sorrel.

090
GLIFFAES COUNTRY HOUSE HOTEL

Crickhowell, Powys NP8 1RH

01874 730 371
www.gliffaeshotel.com

I n a world of grey, wouldn't it be good to discover somewhere colourful? Somewhere where the friendliness is genuine? A place where spas and gyms can't begin to compete with a walk in the Black Mountains or an evening of fishing on the river Usk. Welcome to Gliffaes; 33 unspoilt acres on the banks of the river Usk in the Brecon Beacons National Park. Gliffaes was awarded a Visit Wales Gold Award for 2011, Good Hotel Guide Cesar award in 2009 and is the only four star hotel in the National Park.

Half the pleasure of going away for a day or two is to enjoy good food and wine in an unhurried and pleasant atmosphere without too much fuss and pretention. James and Susie Suter were the ones to create this atmosphere at Gliffaes but Head Chef Karl Cheetham has done his part in keeping guests very happy in the dining room. Blessed with so much fresh, local, high quality produce, including some from the hotel's gardens and orchard, Karl has given the food at Gliffaes a modern British style with a classical French influence. Being a hotel means we do more than just lunch and dinner. Gliffaes is well known for its afternoon teas and makes a perfect wedding or party venue. The location really cannot be beaten. Gliffaes has splendid private dining facilities and people who throw elaborate parties delight Karl and his team when they are challenged with requests for special menus.

The fact that so many people return to Gliffaes year in, year out speaks volumes for the high standards maintained by Karl and his team in the Gliffaes kitchen.

Blessed with so much fresh, local, high quality produce, including some from the hotel's gardens and orchard, Karl has given the food at Gliffaes a modern British style with a classical French influence

CRISP DUCK EGG WITH WILD MUSHROOM MOUSSE & PICKLED MUSHROOM

SERVES 6

2010 Camel Valley Bacchus Dry, Cornwall

Ingredients

Crisp Duck Egg

6 duck eggs
225g fresh white breadcrumbs
2 hen eggs
flour for coating

Pickled Mushrooms

20 small button mushrooms (peeled)
300ml white wine
225g mixed wild mushrooms (any of the following are suitable: Oyster, Enoki, Golden Enoki, Pink Oyster, Buna Shimeji or Shiro Shimeji)
100ml water
300ml white wine vinegar
200g Usk Valley clear Honey
4 bay leaves
1 large pinch pickling spice
1 pinch Sichuan pepper

Wild Mushroom Mousse

170g dried wild mushrooms
340g fresh wild mushrooms
1 onion (finely chopped)
2 cloves garlic (finely chopped)
1 small bunch thyme
85g unsalted butter
1 shot brandy
3 slices whole meal bread
142 ml double cream
75g vegetarian gelatine powder

Method

For the crisp duck eggs

Fill a large pan with water and bring to the boil.

Gently place duck eggs in the pan and simmer for about 2½ minutes. Place the eggs in a bowl of iced water until they have cooled. While the duck eggs are cooling, whisk the hens' eggs in a small bowl.

Once the duck eggs are completely cool, peel them, coat them in the beaten hens' eggs and roll in flour and breadcrumbs.

The eggs can then be deep fried until golden brown before serving.

For the pickled mushrooms

Place all the liquid ingredients into a saucepan and add the spices. Bring the mixture to the boil then whisk in the honey and season. Take off the heat and leave to cool.

Prepare the mushrooms. Cut the stems off the button mushrooms and peel off the skins to help them to absorb the pickled flavour. The larger of the wild mushrooms can be cut in half down the stems.

Pour the liquid ingredients over the mushrooms, put the mixture into a kilner jar and seal. Put the jar in the fridge and leave for at least 24 hours. The mushrooms will then last for 2-3 weeks if kept refrigerated.

For the wild mushroom mousse

Put the dried mushrooms in a large saucepan and cover with one pint of water, then add a pinch of vegetable bouillon and boil until soft.

Drain the liquid from the mushroom and put into a jug. Reserve for later.

Gently fry the garlic, onions and thyme in a large frying pan.

Once the onion mixture is soft, add the dried and fresh mushrooms, cream and the liquid from the dried mushrooms.

Allow the mixture to gently boil until the liquid has reduced by half. Pour the mixture into a liquidiser and blend. Once the mixture is a liquid, pour through a sieve to make sure it is completely smooth.

Add the gelatine and pour into a shallow tray. Cover with clingfilm and shelve in the fridge to set.

To serve

Assemble as in the picture.

LOIN OF WELSH VENISON, SAVOY CABBAGE, WARM ORANGE, THYME & SMOKED BACON, BREAD & BUTTER PUDDING, SMOKED CHESTNUT PUREE

SERVES 4-6

🍷 *2006 Bishop Shiraz – Ben Glaetzer, Barossa Valley Australia*

Ingredients

4-6 x 170g Venison Loin Pieces

Bread and Butter Pudding

250g unsalted butter
250g smoked pancetta
300ml double cream
50ml milk
1 medium loaf white bread (slightly stale)
1 bunch thyme
4 large oranges
6 egg yolks
honey

Smoked Chestnut Purée

200g smoked chestnuts
1 small onion (finely chopped)
1 small leek (finely chopped)
1 clove garlic (finely chopped)
200ml cream
100ml chicken stock

Method

For the bread and butter pudding

Cut the crusts off the bread (reserving for use as breadcrumbs) and butter one side of each slice.

Put the cream and milk into a large bowl. Zest and juice two of the oranges and add to the cream. Segment the remaining oranges and add to the mix.

Take the leaves off the thyme, chop and add them to the mix.

Put the egg yolks into another bowl and, while whisking, slowly add the cream mix to the yolks. When it is all mixed, add 3 – 4 large dessert spoons of honey and season.

Prepare a greased tray (15 x 7 inches & 6 inches deep).

Finely dice the onions and cut the bacon into small strips. Cook the bacon and onion together in a frying pan with a little butter until they start to brown. Remove from the heat and drain to remove any grease. Now you can start to make your pudding.

Evenly pour some of the cream mix into the tray to cover the bottom. Then add a layer of buttered bread, butter side up, then take half the bacon and evenly spread across the bread. Continue until you have three layers of bread, two of bacon and you have added all of the cream mix. Place a sheet of greaseproof paper directly on top of the pudding, then cover the tray with tin foil and place in the oven heated to Gas mark 3 or 160°C for 30 minutes or until you can see it starting to soufflé (you don't want it as wet or soft as you would make it for a pudding). After removing it from the oven, take a tray or baking sheet that will fit inside the pudding tray and press it down with something heavy.

For the venison

Pan-fry the venison pieces in a hot pan then put the pan in the oven for 7 minutes at 190°C. Rest the meat for five minutes

For the smoked chestnut purée

Fry the onions, garlic and leeks in a large pan then add the chicken stock, chestnuts and cream. Boil the mixture until the liquid has reduced by about half. The mixture can then be blended to a smooth purée.

To serve

Serve the venison with the bread and butter pudding, seasonal vegetables, a light sauce and the chestnut purée.

TRIO OF RHUBARB (ICE CREAM SANDWICH, SORBET & SHERBET)

SERVES 6

2005 Château de la Chartreuse , Sauternes

Ingredients

Parfait

570ml double cream
5 large eggs (separated)
1 tbsp caster sugar
2 tbsp brandy
85g caster sugar
2 vanilla pods

Rhubarb Jelly

500g rhubarb (chopped)
125g caster sugar
5 sheets leaf gelatine

Biscuit

115g butter
225g plain flour
225g caster sugar
7 egg whites

Sherbet

200g white chocolate
150ml double cream (whipped)
1 rhubarb (dried and powdered)
4 tbsp icing sugar
1 tbsp cream of tartar
1 tbsp bicarbonate of soda

Method

For the parfait

Separate the eggs and whisk the egg yolks.

In a heatproof bowl, whisk the egg yolks, brandy and a tablespoon of caster sugar over a pan of simmering water until thick and frothy. This is a called a sabayon.

Next whisk the egg whites and 85g of caster sugar until they form stiff peaks. In another bowl whisk the cream.

You now need to combine all of the ingredients. Take a large bowl and gently fold the egg whites, sabayon and cream together. Add about 1/3 of each at a time until it is combined.

Finally, spread the mixture carefully onto a shallow tray and freeze.

For the rhubarb jelly

Put the chopped rhubarb, caster sugar and ½ tablespoon of water into a saucepan and cook over a low heat until soft.

While the rhubarb is cooking, soak the gelatine sheets in a bowl of water until they are soft.

Once the rhubarb and gelatine are both ready blend them together and spread the mixture into a shallow tray and then put in the fridge to set.

For the biscuits

In a large bowl, cream the butter and sugar together. Then add half the flour and mix until combined. Repeat with the other half. Finally, add the eggs whites slowly and blend.

Set the mixture aside in the fridge until you are ready to prepare the ice cream sandwich.

For the sherbet

To make dried rhubarb, divide each stick into four inch long pieces and then slice each piece into thin slithers. Carefully brush the rhubarb slithers in sugar syrup and then dry in a warm place or in the oven on a very low heat. Then blend them to a fine powder. Melt white chocolate in a large, heat-proof bowl. Gently fold the whipped cream into the melted chocolate followed by roughly ½ of the rhubarb powder.

Put the chocolate mixture into the fridge to set. The mixture will not become solid but once it is firm you can roll the mix into small balls. Place to one side while you make the sherbet.

In a large bowl, mix the icing sugar, cream of tartar, bicarbonate of soda and the rest of the rhubarb powder. You can now roll the prepared chocolate through the sherbet.

To serve

Add the rhubarb parfait and jelly between two biscuits to make the ice cream sandwich.

THE HAND AT LLARNAMON

Llanarmon Dyffryn Ceiriog, Ceiriog Valley, Llangollen LL20 7LD

01691 600 666
www.thehandhotel.co.uk

The margins between England and Wales have been fought over for centuries-and for good reason! Apart from any economic or strategic considerations, this is stunning countryside. Who wouldn't want to claim it for their own?

The Ceiriog Valley occupies an almost mythical status within this most romantic of areas of the British Isles. It is known as the Valley of the Poets, having inspired artists for generations. John Ceiriog Hughes, the 'Welsh Shakespeare', lived in Llanarmon and drew inspiration from the breathtaking landscape of the Upper Ceiriog Valley.

Small wonder then that the kitchen brigade at The Hand at Llanarmon, whom breathe this air every day, dream up some of the best dishes to be found in Wales today.

Head Chef Mulholland uses local produce for environmental reasons, of course, but as much because a finer larder would be hard to find anywhere in the world. Sheep and cattle raised in lush, green valleys and matured on the wild uplands produce some of the finest lamb and beef you're ever likely to sink your teeth into. There's also fresh pheasant when it is in season and trout to write home about.

The inn was acquired by Gaynor and Martin De Luchi in 2003 and they were quickly joined by Grant Mulholland as Head Chef, who has been with them ever since and shares their vision of superb food served with flair, generosity and a minimum of fuss.

Add to this a well-stocked bar which embraces all-comers, comfortable en-suite bedrooms, blazing log fires on colder days and a sun-lit terrace for summer dog-days, and you have the quintessential British inn.

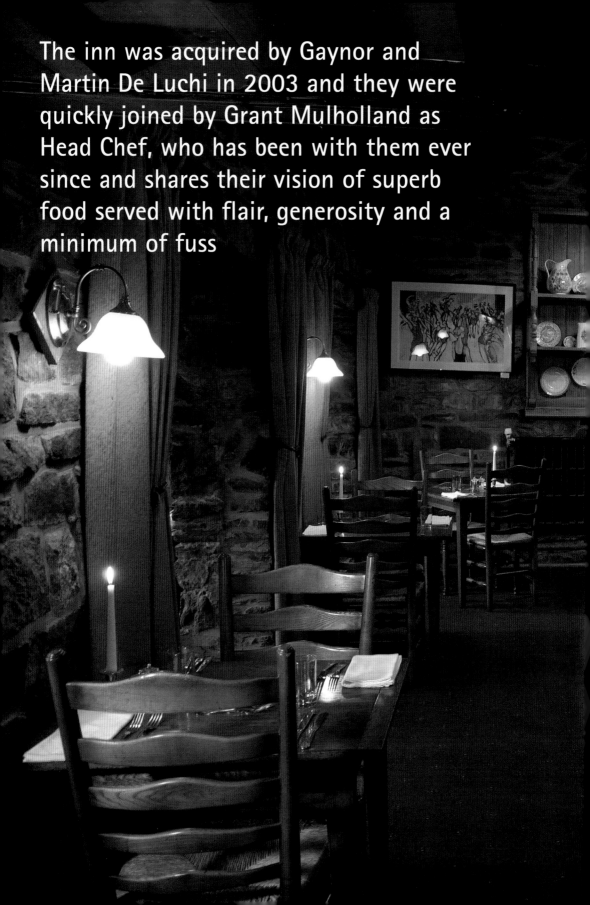

The inn was acquired by Gaynor and Martin De Luchi in 2003 and they were quickly joined by Grant Mulholland as Head Chef, who has been with them ever since and shares their vision of superb food served with flair, generosity and a minimum of fuss

LLYN PENINSULA CRAB SPRING ROLL WITH A SMOKED TROUT PARMESAN SNAP

SERVES 4-6

 Domaine de Boulay,
Sauvignon de Touraine

Ingredients

400g oak-smoked trout
juice of ½ lemon
150g parmesan
200g filo pastry sheets
50g white crab meat
2cm piece fresh ginger
50g samphire
½ fresh cauliflower
20g butter
100ml milk
½ onion
40g micro herbs
1 egg
2 tsp olive oil
salt and freshly ground black pepper

Method

Start by preheating the oven to 180°C.

Finely chop the cauliflower and soften in melted butter for 2 – 3 minutes. Add the finely chopped onion and enough milk to barely cover the mixture. Cook until soft. Strain the mixture and retain the liquid, then liquidise, adding a little milk if required.

Lay out a sheet of greaseproof paper. Finely grate the fresh parmesan and, using a 5cm cutter, portion into rings on the paper. Bake for 5 – 6 minutes or until just bubbling. When nearly set, remove from the paper and loosely wrap around a wooden spoon handle to form a parmesan snap. Leave to cool. Flake the smoked trout with lemon juice and seasoning. Use this mixture to fill the parmesan snap.

Gently fry the samphire, grated fresh ginger and crab meat in a little butter. To make the spring roll, place a double layer of filo pastry – approximately 15cm square – on a clean surface. Place a spoonful of the crab mixture on the bottom third of the pastry, fold in the sides and roll. Seal the edges with beaten egg and deep-fry for 5 – 8 minutes until crisp.

Dress the micro herbs with a little olive oil.

To serve

Assemble as in the picture.

CEIRIOG VALLEY PHEASANT CASSEROLE WITH A SMOKED SHALLOT & TARRAGON SAUCE

SERVES 2

Les Garrigues, Domaine Clavel, from the Languedoc

Ingredients

1 pheasant (cut into 4 portions)
100g smoked bacon
1 bulb smoked garlic
225g shallots
1 bunch fresh tarragon
2 tbsp olive oil
500ml chicken stock
25g flour
200ml Cassis
200ml red wine
salt, freshly ground black pepper

Brussels sprouts with Parmesan

350g Brussels sprouts
25g butter
1 clove garlic
100g parmesan
salt, freshly ground black pepper

Traditional Bread Sauce

500ml milk
50g butter
1 onion
6 cloves, 6 peppercorns, 1 bay leaf, 1 sprig thyme
150g white breadcrumbs
3 tbsp single cream
pinch nutmeg

Straw Potatoes

400g potatoes
few sprigs fresh rosemary

Method

Preheat the oven to 180°C. Heat the oil in a heavy frying pan and evenly brown the pheasant portions. Remove them from the pan and place in a lidded, oven-proof casserole dish.

In the same frying pan, sauté the chopped shallots and bacon and then add the finely chopped smoked garlic. Remove from the pan and set to one side.

Add enough flour to soak up the juices in the frying pan and mix well. Add the red wine, roughly torn tarragon, chicken stock and Cassis and, stirring continuously, bring slowly to the boil. Add the sautéed shallots, bacon and garlic and cook for 5 minutes before pouring over the pheasant portions.

Place the covered casserole in the oven and cook for one and a half hours, or until tender.

For the brussels sprouts with parmesan

Gently heat the butter in a pan. Add the finely sliced Brussels sprouts and cook until just soft. Add the freshly grated parmesan, check the seasoning and serve immediately.

For the traditional bread sauce

In a pan, gently simmer the milk, butter, chopped onion, cloves, peppercorns, thyme and bay leaf for 10 – 15 minutes. Strain the liquid and return to the pan. Add the breadcrumbs, single cream, nutmeg and seasoning. Cook gently for a further 5 minutes and serve.

For the straw potatoes

Peel the potatoes and cut into fine matchsticks no more than 0.5cm in thickness. Leave in cold water.

Pre-heat a deep-fat fryer to 180°C. Drain the potato matchsticks and pat dry with kitchen paper. Fry the matchsticks until crisp and lightly golden brown. Add the rosemary sprigs for the final 30 seconds.

Drain and place on kitchen paper to absorb any excess oil.

To serve

Assemble as in the picture.

VANILLA AND DARK CHOCOLATE BAVAROIS WITH ICED LEMON CURD AND BASIL SHORTBREAD

SERVES 6-8

🍷 *Moscato d'Asti, Vigna Senza Nome, Giacomo Bologna*

Ingredients

Makes 8 70mm rings

Vanilla and Dark Chocolate Bavarois

seeds from 2 vanilla pods
4 egg yolks
few drops good vanilla extract
125g caster sugar
500ml milk
25g leaf gelatine
500ml whipping cream
180g good dark chocolate

Iced Lemon Curd

2 lemons (zest and juice)
100g caster sugar
50g butter
2 eggs

Basil Shortbread

80g butter
20g icing sugar
1 egg white
140g plain flour
4 leaves fresh basil

Method

Preheat the oven to 160°C

For the vanilla and dark chocolate bavarois

Mix the egg yolks and sugar in a large bowl. Heat the milk with the vanilla pod seeds and vanilla extract then add this and mix well, but without making the mixture frothy. Place the bowl over a pan of boiling water and stir until the mixture coats the back of the spoon. Soak the leaf gelatine in cold water, drain, and stir into the vanilla mixture until completely dissolved. Pass through a strainer into a fresh bowl and stand the bowl in a container of iced water. Stir until the mixture is at setting point and divide the mixture into 2 halves.

Melt the chocolate over a bowl of hot water and add to half of the vanilla mixture. Stir until completely mixed.

Lightly whip the cream and fold half into each of the chocolate and vanilla mixtures.

Fill one third of each of the rings with the vanilla mixture. Repeat with the chocolate mixture and finish with a layer of the vanilla mixture. Leave to set.

For the iced lemon curd

Put the lemon zest, lemon juice, sugar and butter into a bowl. Set over a pan of gently simmering water and stir until the butter has melted. Whisk in the eggs and continue to whisk until the mixture thickens. Leave to cool then place in a freezer.

For the basil shortbread

In a bowl, mix the butter, icing sugar and egg white. Add the flour, salt and 4 finely chopped basil leaves. Chill for 30 minutes. Place the mixture between 2 sheets of greaseproof paper and roll out to a thickness of approximately 4mm. Remove paper and cut into 5cm squares. Bake for 8 – 10 minutes until lightly golden.

To serve

Assemble as in the picture.

110
THE HARDWICK

Old Raglan Road, Abergavenny, Monmouthshire NP7 9AA

01873 854 220
www.thehardwick.co.uk

The Hardwick has become a serious gastronomic destination since beginning life as a country pub in the 1800's. After being taken over by Stephen Terry and his wife, Joanna, in 2005 it has been transformed from being a dated roadside pub into a Five Star Visit Wales accredited Restaurant with Rooms. The Hardwick has eight luxury bedrooms set in a peaceful annexe; a large bar area; extended dining rooms and also benefits from a private dining facility. Having learnt his craft alongside Michel Roux and Marco Pierre White, Stephen Terry has developed an ethos of simple food cooked well or 'Ronseal' cooking as he likes to call it ("It does what it says on the menu"). Quality ingredients are locally sourced as far as possible and are accompanied by local draught beers and an extensive wine list, all served in a relaxed, comfortable atmosphere. Stephen has designed the lengthy menu to be all things to all people, incorporating contemporary dishes as well as old favourites such as beer battered cod or 21 day aged rib-eye steak.

The Hardwick is not an occasional fine dining restaurant, our aim is to deliver consistently good quality food at good value for money with friendly, efficient service in an unpretentious environment. We let our guests bring their own occasions

PORK BELLY AND BLACK PUDDING, APPLE & MUSTARD WITH LOBSTER, BROWN BUTTER, DANDELION AND PEA SHOOTS

SERVES 4

 *Meursault or Chablis*

Ingredients

750g pork belly
250g ring black pudding (finely sliced)
2 x 500g live lobsters
20g flour, for dusting
80-100g fresh breadcrumbs
2 free-range eggs
100ml rapeseed oil
25g pea shoots
25g dandelion leaves

Apple Purée

2 Bramley apples (peeled, cores removed and finely chopped)
25g caster sugar, 1 tsp English mustard, pinch of salt to season
Heat and mix all the the apples, sugar, mustard and salt until it purees.

Lobster Sauce

100g salted butter
20g small capers
15g picked flat parsley (chopped)

Salad Dressing

1 unwaxed lemon (juiced)
100ml extra virgin olive oil
Mix together to make dressing

Method

For the pork belly

Preheat the oven to 140°C. Place the pork belly into a large roasting tray and add enough water to reach half-way up the sides of the pork. Cut out a rectangle of greaseproof paper the size of the pork belly and cover the pork belly with it. Cover the roasting tray with a double layer of aluminium foil, sealing well.

Transfer the pork belly to the oven and cook for eight hours, or until tender and falling apart. Carefully remove the pork from the cooking liquid and set aside to cool slightly, fat-side facing upwards. (Reserve the cooking liquid).

Discard the skin and reserve the fat in a large mixing bowl. Pick the pork belly meat from the bones and sinew. Add the pork belly meat to the underbelly fat and mix until well combined (this will keep it moist when you reheat it).

Arrange one third of the black pudding slices side-by-side on a baking tray. Add a 1cm layer of pork belly meat. Top with another layer of black pudding. Repeat the layering process until all of the black pudding and pork belly meat has been used up and the layers are 4cm thick. Wrap clingfilm tightly around the baking tray and black pudding and pork belly layers, then chill in the fridge for at least four hours, or until set.

For the lobsters

Place the lobsters into simmering water for 5 minutes. Remove then pick the meat from the tail and claws. Cut each tail into six and the claws in half.

For the lobster sauce

Heat the butter until it starts to brown, add the capers with a little caper juice and parsley. Clingfilm and keep warm. When the black pudding and pork belly layers have set, cut into 6cm x 4cm rectangles. Dredge each rectangle of pork and black pudding first in the flour, then dip them in the beaten egg, then finally roll them in the breadcrumbs until coated.

Heat a third of the rapeseed oil in a frying pan over a medium heat. Add the black pudding and pork belly rectangles, in batches, and fry for 4-5 minutes on each side, or until crisp and golden-brown. Repeat this using the remaining rapeseed oil. Transfer the fried black pudding and pork belly rectangles to the oven (160°C) and continue to cook for 4-5 minutes, or until heated through. Cut into three to serve. Once cooled, stir in about one tablespoon of English mustard. Chill in the fridge until needed.

To serve

Place the warmed belly pieces and lobster on the plate. Dress the belly with the apple sauce, the lobster with the caper butter and garnish with salad dressing, dressed dandelion and pea shoots.

A TASTE OF RABBIT

SERVES 4

 Côte Rotie

Ingredients

Loin
2 loins of rabbit
6 slices of Parma ham
100g chicken breast
livers, heart and kidneys of rabbit (offal)
20ml double cream
1 tsp sherry vinegar
salt and pepper

Scotch Egg
2 rabbit legs (minced)
4 quail eggs
1 egg white
30g flour
100g dry breadcrumbs
salt and pepper

Pithiver
2 rabbit shoulders
150g pancetta (sliced)
5g parsley
50g butter
50g plain flour
200ml rabbit stock (see below)
1 roll of puff pastry
2 egg yolks

Rabbit Stock
1 rabbit carcass (roasted)
1 small carrot
1 stick of celery
1 small leek
1 small onion
Chop the bones and roast for 10-15 minutes at 180°C.
Place the bones and all the stock vegetables into a stockpot. Cover with water and cook over a medium heat for 2-3 hours. Strain and cool..

Method

Break the rabbit carcasses down each into 2 shoulders, 2 legs, 2 loins and the offal. Your butcher can do this for you, but don't forget to ask for the bones back for the stock.

For the pithiver

While the stock is cooking, wrap the rabbit shoulders in muslin and place in the simmering stock to braise for 90 minutes. Then remove from the stock and pull all the meat from the shoulders. Set aside.

Fry the pancetta to colour in a heavy-based pan. Remove the pancetta but keep the fat. Add the butter to this and then add the flour to make a roux. Add some of the rabbit stock to create a thick sauce then mix in the chopped parsley, pancetta, shoulder meat. Correct the seasoning. Leave to cool then shape into four patties.

Cut 8 discs from the pastry using a 5cm ring. Brush 4 discs with egg yolk and place a meat patty on each. Top with the remaining discs and seal the pastry edges. Score the top of each pithiver and refrigerate.

For the scotch egg

Mince the rabbit legs and season. Boil the quail eggs for 2 minutes, refresh in ice water, peel and pat dry. Make a patty using a quarter of the mince in one hand, and use to cover an egg. Repeat to make 4. Now roll each meat-wrapped egg first in the flour, then in lightly whisked egg white and then coat in breadcrumbs. Refrigerate.

For the loin

Blitz the chicken breast to form a smooth paste in a food processor, adding the cream, salt and pepper then chill. Sauté the offal for 3 minutes over a medium heat. When cooked through, remove from the pan and deglaze with sherry vinegar. Leave to cool. Then blitz in a food processor and stir into to the chicken mixture.

Cut a length of clingfilm 30% longer than the length of the rabbit loin. Overlap the Parma ham slices on the clingfilm. Thinly spread the chicken mousse over two thirds of the ham (in the centre). Now place the loins in the centre of the mousse and roll up tightly. Chill to set.

To serve

Reduce the rabbit stock by two thirds for gravy. Cook the loin in a waterbath at 65°C for 15 minutes, remove the clingfilm and seal the outside in a hot frying pan. Leave to rest. Bake the pithivers at 160°C for 13 minutes until golden. Deep-fry the scotch egg for 3-4 minutes in a fryer at 180°C. Slice the rolled loin into 8 slices. Plate each dish with 2 slices of loin, one pithiver and a scotch egg. Serve with the gravy in a sauceboat.

RELISH WALES
THE HARDWICK

A PLATE OF CHOCOLATE LOVELINESS

SERVES 6-8

 *Recioto della Valpolicella*

Ingredients

Chocolate Mousse

90g 75% dark chocolate (chopped)
90g 32% milk chocolate (chopped)
100g butter (softened),130g egg yolks,
125g egg whites

Millionaire Shortbread

75g butter (softened), 115g plain flour,
30g cornflour
60g caster sugar
½ tsp. (each) baking powder, sea salt,
vanilla extract

Caramel

1 can condensed milk, 3 tbsp golden syrup
1 tbsp dark muscovado sugar
200g butter
Add all the caramel ingredients stirring
continuously, over a medium heat.
Remove pan and add pinch of salt.

Chocolate Topping

250g dark chocolate (melt in bain-marie)

Brownie

288g butter
345g dark muscovado sugar
230g whole eggs
160g 70% dark chocolate
130g plain flour
15g cocoa,½ tsp salt, 10g vanilla sugar

Parfait

125g sugar
½ cup water
6 egg yolks
500g double cream
150g strawberry jam,150g peanut butter

Method

For the chocolate mousse

Melt the chocolate over a bain-marie in a metal bowl. Add the butter and stir until melted, then add the egg yolks. The mixture will become thick and shiny. In a separate bowl, beat the egg whites to create soft peaks and then fold into the chocolate mixture. Transfer to a clean bowl and refrigerate to set for 24 hours.

For shortbread crumble

Add the butter and vanilla extract to the sieved dry ingredients, and rub, using fingertips, to make breadcrumbs. Tip mix onto a baking tray and cook at 160°C for 15-20 minutes until golden. Cool, then break up into a bowl. Melt a knob of butter and mix into the crumble. Pack the mixture firmly into the base of the tin to make a layer approximately. ½ cm thick. Refrigerate for 20 minutes to set.

For the caramel

Pour the caramel over the shortbread crumble base. Return to the fridge and leave it to set for 4-6 hours. Now pour over the melted dark chocolate topping. Once again, return to the fridge to set.

For the brownie

Cream the butter and sugar. Melt the chocolate (bain-marie) and then add the egg yolks. Mix together until the chocolate becomes thick and shiny, then fold into the creamed butter and sugar. Fold in the sieved dry ingredients. Line a shallow rectangular baking tin with baking parchment and spread the mixture evenly in the tin. Bake for 25-30 minutes at 170°C. Chill in the fridge, then remove the brownie from the tin and lay between 2 sheets of greaseproof paper. Use a rolling pin to flatten the brownie (1.5 cm thick). Line a 2lb loaf tin with clingfilm and greaseproof paper, ensuring there's enough overhang to wrap over the finished parfait. Cut the rolled brownie, and press into the base of the loaftin, to fit snugly. Spread a thin layer of jam over the brownie base. Set aside.

For the parfait

Whisk the egg yolks to form a creamy colour. Set aside. Heat the sugar and water to 118°C ('soft ball'on a sugar thermometer). Pour the syrup over the egg yolks whist continuously whisking. Whisk for a further 3- 5 minutes then add the jam and peanut butter until fully incorporated. In a separate bowl, whip the cream and then gently fold into the egg yolk mix. Pour the parfait on top of the brownie base, level and then wrap over the greaseproof paper and clingfilm to seal. Freeze for 24 hours.

To serve

Assemble as in the picture.

THE IMPERIAL HOTEL

The Promenade, Llandudno, LL30 1AP

01492 877 466
www.theimperial.co.uk

Welcome to Chantrey's Restaurant.
Situated at the heart of the sweeping and stunning promenade of Llandudno Bay lies the impressively elegant, four star Imperial Hotel and its highly recommended, AA Rosette-Awarded Chantrey's Restaurant.
Named after Samuel Chantrey, the original and distinguished owner of The Imperial Hotel, Chantrey's Restaurant offers diners a relaxing, friendly and welcoming atmosphere.
Executive Chef Arwel Jones is an active member of the Welsh Culinary Association and a member of the Welsh Salon Culinaire Committee. He is passionate about his homeland and this shows in everything he does, from speaking Welsh to using Welsh produce in the kitchen alongside Head Chef Joanne Williams. They use the finest local, seasonal and market-fresh produce of all kinds, from unique cheeses and wines; Welsh lamb and beef; and fresh fish and seafood because of its distinctiveness, quality and taste. Diners will therefore find a mouth-watering and imaginative à la Carte menu, which includes Arwel's hugely popular signature dishes, and have the flexibility of choosing from one course or two, up to a full dining experience. In addition, Chantrey's has a daily "Special" menu as well as a superb Traditional Sunday Lunch. The hotel also endeavours to arrange a meal according not only to special dietary requirements, but also any particular favourite dishes. So one can see why it won the

prestigious AA Hotel of the Year Wales 2010-11 Award and can rightfully boast an outstanding reputation for food and service. Diners can also enjoy a relaxing drink before and after dinner in the hotel's bar and on the attractive veranda, which has the most spectacular views across Llandudno bay, with Wales' longest pier and the Great Orme in all their glory on one side and an outlook stretching to the Little Orme on the other. The Imperial Hotel is the perfect atmosphere in which to soak up those impressive views, while listening to the musical accompaniment of traditional Welsh Harp music or a pianist who is on occasion accompanied by a singer.

Executive Chef Arwel Jones is an active member of the Welsh Culinary Association and a member of the Welsh Salon Culinaire Committee. He is passionate about his homeland and this shows in everything he does, from speaking Welsh to using Welsh produce in the kitchen alongside Head Chef Joanne Williams

TROUT CEVICHE WITH FENNEL

SERVES 4

Sauvignon Blanc - Lutzville Cape Diamond Vineyards, Olifants River, South Africa

Ingredients

Trout

4 local trout fillets (skinned and pinned)
300ml lemon juice
300ml lime juice
100g sugar
1 bunch of dill (chopped)

Fennel

2 fennel bulbs
570ml fish stock
200ml white wine

Cucumber Granite and Jelly

4 cucumbers
1 shot of vodka
4 leaves of gelatine
salt and pepper
1 lemon

baby cress for garnish

Method

For the trout ceviche

Mix the lemon and lime juice, chopped dill and sugar together. Pour over the trout fillets and leave in the fridge for 10-12 hours.

For the cucumber granite and jelly

Cut the cucumbers down the middle and take out all of the seeds. Roughly chop them and place in a food blender and blitz for a couple of minutes. Dissolve the gelatine in cold water. Press the cucumber mix through a fine cloth and split in half. With one half, add the vodka, store in a container and freeze, mixing occasionally to keep it slushy. With the other half, warm up a little, add the squeezed gelatine to dissolve and add a squeeze of lemon juice and leave to set in a tray.

For the fennel

Cut up the fennel into very fine shreds and poach in the fish stock and wine for about 10 minutes. Drain and cool.

To serve

Arrange the fennel down the middle of the plate. Place the trout fillet on top, cut jelly into cubes and arrange around the plate. Fill the tall shot glass with granite. Complete the dish with baby cress.

TRIO OF WELSH LAMB

SERVES 4

 *Tanners Claret, Bordeaux, France*

Ingredients

Lamb Shoulder

500g Welsh lamb shoulder
1 carrot, leek and onion
1 head of celery (chopped)
1 bunch of fresh rosemary
300ml red wine
150g redcurrant jelly
8 slices of prosciutto ham or Carmarthen ham

Lamb Faggots

350g minced Welsh lamb
75g Welsh lambs liver
2 free range eggs beaten
75g fresh breadcrumbs
handful of chopped fresh sage and rosemary
salt and pepper
250g caul fat
500g chicken stock

Lamb Loin

1 Welsh lamb loin
100g fresh breadcrumbs
1 bunch of fresh mint (chopped)

Fondant Potato

4 large potatoes (peeled)
300ml chicken stock
200g butter

Shallots

4 shallots
50g brown sugar
100ml balsamic vinegar

200g garden peas
½ savoy cabbage
1 carrot
4 baby carrot

Method

For the lamb shoulder

Dice up the lamb shoulder, carrot, leek, celery and onion in a roasting tray. Add the rosemary, red wine and redcurrant jelly then slow-cook in a preheated oven at 150°C for approximately 5-6 hours. Strain off the sauce in the tray, keeping it to finish the dish. Flake the lamb shoulder, mixing it well with the vegetables. Season and wrap in the ham. Leave to cool and set in the fridge. Reheat when ready to serve.

For the faggots

Mix the lamb mince, liver, eggs, breadcrumbs and herbs in a bowl. Add seasoning, roll into medium size balls and wrap in the caul fat. Seal in hot oil to colour and poach in the chicken stock for 30 minutes.

For the lamb loin

Cut off all the fat and sinew and cut into 4 equal portions. Seal in hot oil and cook for 5-6 minutes, leaving it to rest. Mix the breadcrumbs and chopped mint. Roll in the minted crumb and warm in the oven just before serving.

For the fondant potato

Cut the potatoes into squares and cook in the chicken stock and butter.

For the pea purée

Cook the peas in salted water then strain and blitz with a little butter in a blender until smooth.

For the cabbage and carrot

Finely shred and chop the cabbage, dice the carrot and cook in butter until soft. Season.

For the shallots

Peel shallots removing all the outer skin. Mix with the brown sugar and balsamic vinegar and cook in the oven until golden brown.

For the baby carrots

Blanch in salted water.

To serve

Place the lamb loin on the cabbage and lay the faggot on the potato. Then add the shoulder and finish with shallots, pea purée, baby carrot and left over sauce from the shoulder.

CHOCOLATE AND MERLIN TORTE WITH PECAN ICE CREAM

SERVES 4

🍷 *Muscat de St-Jean-de Minervois, Vignerons de Septimanie, France*

Ingredients

Chocolate Sponge

5 free range eggs
100g caster sugar
75g plain flour
30g cocoa powder

Chocolate Mousse

450g dark chocolate
250ml egg whites
200g caster sugar (boil to soft ball - 240°C)
5 gelatine leaves
600ml semi whipped double cream
75ml Welsh merlin liqueur

Coffee Jelly

300ml strong latte coffee
4 leaves of gelatine
50g sugar

Caramel Sauce

200g caster sugar
100ml double cream
40g butter

Ice Cream

200ml milk
200ml double cream
60g caster sugar
4 egg yolks
100g pecan nuts
1 vanilla pod

50g pecan nuts to garnish

Method

For the chocolate sponge

Whisk eggs and sugar until light and fluffy. Fold in flour and coco powder. Cook on a lined flat tray and bake in a pre-heated oven at 180°C for approximately 10 to 15 minutes. Cool and cut to fit four moulds.

For the mousse

Soften the gelatine in cold water. Melt the chocolate. Whip the egg whites until light and fluffy and add the soft ball sugar. Squeeze the gelatine and dissolve in the heat of the sugar pan and add to the egg white mix. Fold in the semi whipped cream into the melted chocolate, then fold into the egg white mix and add the Welsh Merlin liqueur. Set in the moulds lined with the chocolate sponge and leave to set in the fridge.

For the coffee jelly

Soften the gelatine in cold water then squeeze. Dissolve in the warm coffee. Leave to cool and then pour over the mousse in the moulds. Pour a little into a flat tray to use as garnish.

For the ice cream

Place milk, cream, vanilla and half of the sugar into a pan and bring to the boil. Whisk the egg yolk and remaining sugar in a bowl and pour over the milk mixture. Strain into a clean pan and cook until it thickens. Chill then churn in an ice cream machine and finish with chopped pecans and ripple with a little caramel sauce.

For the caramel sauce

Put the sugar in a heavy-based pan then stir in 4 tablespoons of water. Bring to the boil until you have caramel. Take off the heat, carefully stir in the cream and butter, then cool.

To serve

Place a torte on the plate with the ice cream and garnish with the left over jelly, pecan nuts and caramel sauce.

130
THE KINMEL ARMS

The Village, St George, Nr Abergele, Conwy LL22 9BP

01745 832 207
www.kinmelarms.co.uk

Situated between the mountains and the sea, St George is a secluded hamlet overlooking the North Wales coast and this is where you will find The Kinmel Arms. Tim and Lynn purchased this building on 14th February 2002 with the vision of creating a deliciously peaceful place in which to eat, rest and explore. This romantic quest, along with plenty of hard work, has evolved over the years into the uniqueness that is The Kinmel Arms today.

The 17th century sandstone walls and mullion windows on the outside are a contrast to the clean, contemporary and eclectic spaces on the inside, that are enlivened by Tim's artworks. Buzzy brasserie style lunches and then a la carte evening meals are served in a relaxed dining atmosphere, everything you would expect from a 5 star restaurant with rooms with such wonderful produce on offer from North Wales and Cheshire.

The restaurant has collected many awards over the years and Head Chef Gwyn Roberts's menus reflect years of training in some of the top restaurants in Britain. The team produce dishes with flair and flavour, so expect taste buds to be challenged, delighted and rewarded. The bar serves local real ales and Welsh ciders, and has a wide selection of spirits. The wine list visits many unusual parts or the world and offers twenty one wines by the glass.

The four suites available to guests are divine with super king sized beds, Egyptian linen, porcelain bathrooms and their own quiet style. Overall, The Kinmel Arms is the place to unwind.

The team produce dishes with flair and flavour, so expect taste buds to be challenged, delighted and rewarded. The bar serves local real ales and Welsh ciders, and has a wide selection of spirits. The wine list visits many unusual parts or the world and offers twenty one wines by the glass

OVEN-ROAST QUAIL, POTATO NEST, PUMPKIN PURÉE, APPLE TEMPURA, PUY AND A VANILLA AND WELSH LIQUEUR JUS

SERVES 4

Moko Black, Pinot Noir, Otago, New Zealand 2009

Ingredients

4 whole dressed quail (wishbone and feet removed)
2 Maris Piper potatoes (peeled but not washed)
1 pumpkin
1 Granny Smith apple
100g butter
10g five-spice powder

For the dressing

100g Puy lentils (soaked overnight in cold water)
1 carrot, 1 swede (peeled and finely diced)
1 bay leaf
1 rasher smoked bacon
100ml chicken stock
50ml olive oil

For the jus

200ml red wine
50ml port
100g redcurrant jelly
1 vanilla pod
20ml Welsh Aronia berry liqueur

For the tempura batter

50g plain flour
50ml soda water

Method

For the quail

Pan-fry each breast until golden brown then place the whole birds into an oven and roast them for 7-8 minutes at 180°C. Remove from the oven and rest for 5 minutes. Take the quail breasts and legs off the bone with a paring knife.

For the jus

Place the quail bones in a pan and cook until browned. Add the vegetable trimmings, red wine, port, liqueur, redcurrant jelly and split vanilla pod. Reduce the ingredients to syrup then pass through a fine sieve. Whisk in 30g of unsalted butter into the syrup at the end.

For the pumpkin purée

Cut the pumpkin into large chunks and remove all its seeds. Roast in the oven for 30 minutes at 180°C until soft. Scoop out the cooked flesh and place it into a Thermomix with 50g of butter, salt and pepper. Puree until smooth.

For the potato nests

Using a mandolin, make thin straw sticks of potato. Blanch these in a fryer for 30 seconds at 140°C. Line a ladle with the potato sticks, place another ladle on top to hold them in place and cook them in the fryer for 2-3 minutes at 190°C until crisp. Turn the potato nests out to drain and season them.

For the dressing

Sweat the diced vegetables off in a pan with some butter then drain and add the lentils, diced smoked bacon, bay leaf and chicken stock. Cook for about 15 minutes then cool. Add olive oil and season to taste.

For the tempura batter

Put cold soda water in a bowl and add the flour. Whisk until it becomes frothy.

For the apple

Peel the apple and, using a small ball-cutter, create small spheres of apple. Coat these in five-spice powder and set aside. Prior to serving, dip these in the tempura batter and deep-fry them for 10 seconds at 190°C.

To serve

Place the potato nest in the centre of the plate. Place the quail breasts and legs in the nest. Surround the nest with the pumpkin purée, Puy lentil dressing and five tempura apples. Garnish with apple blossom or micro herbs.

FILLET OF LOCAL WILD TROUT LIGHTLY SMOKED WITH A LOBSTER AND CONWY MUSSEL 'HOT-POT'

SERVES 4

McHenry Hohnen 3 Amigos, Margaret River Australia 2008

Ingredients

2 whole sea trout (gutted, filleted and skinned)
1 local lobster
500g Conwy mussels
100ml white wine
parsley (chopped)

Hot-Pot

pastry - 500g plain flour, 300g butter, pinch salt
1 egg
baking beans for blind baking

Bisque For Lobster

50g butter
2 tbsp tomato puree
1 bulb garlic, 1 bulb fennel
1 onion, 1 leek, 2 star anise
brandy (25ml), vermouth (25ml), pernod (25ml)

Leek Timbale

3 leeks
200ml double cream
50g butter
3 eggs
salt, pepper and nutmeg for seasoning

Saffron Cocotte Potatoes

12 small new potatoes
pinch of quality saffron
30ml Penderyn whisky
20g unsalted butter

Trout mousse

100g trout (tail ends)
1 egg white
50ml double cream
dill (chopped)

For Smoking the Trout

100g oak chippings, 1 lemon rind, 1 grated apple and parchment paper

Method

Cut the trout into 8cm x 6cm rectangles. Place oak chippings, lemon rind and grated apple into a flat pan and cover with parchment paper. Heat them until they are smoking and then add the trout. Cover it with the pan lid then take it off the heat and leave for 2 minutes, set aside.

For the hot-pot

Make up the pastry and then use it to line 4 ramekin pots. Blind-bake with baking beans until they are crisp. Make 4 pot lids with the rest of the pastry brush with egg yolk and bake until they too are crisp.

For the lobster bisque

Cook the lobster for 18 minutes in salted, boiling water. Leave to cool and remove all of the meat. Heat a large pan and add the lobster shell. Cook the shell for 2 minutes and then add the alcohol spirits and flame them down. Add the rest of the ingredients and 500ml of lobster stock. Cook for 30 minutes then pass through a fine sieve. Season with butter

For the potatoes

Trim the potatoes into barrel shapes. Place in boiling, salted water with the saffron and cook them gently until tender. Finish with the whisky and butter to glaze.

For the leek timbale

Line four small ramekin dishes with strips of leek in a patchwork manner. Cut the remaining leeks into a fine dice and sweat down in butter. Then add the cream and cook for 4 minutes. Blend all of this together and then pass through a sieve. Allow to cool then add the eggs and mix them in. Put mixture in the lined ramekins and steam for 14 minutes.

For the conwy mussels

Wash the mussels and remove the beards. Add the white wine and mussels to a hot pan and cook with the lid on until the mussels have opened, then set them aside.

To serve

Place the pastry hot-pot in the oven for 20 seconds then add 50ml of lobster bisque with a generous serving of lobster meat and Conwy mussels.

Heat the hot-pot in the oven for 3 minutes at 180°C. Pan-fry the trout fillets in butter for one and a half minutes on each side. Once cooked, place on kitchen roll to absorb any moisture. Place the timbale, hot-pot and trout fillets on a plate. Spoon the chowder around the plate. Place 3 empty mussel shells on the plate and fill with diced lobster and cocotte potatoes.

We also garnish with trout fillet, Scotch egg and crispy trout skin.

BARA BRITH APPLE CHARLOTTE WITH ORANGE MARMALADE ICE CREAM SERVED IN A WALNUT PRALINE BASKET

SERVES 4

 Late Harvest Sauvignon Blanc, Concha y Toro, Chile

Ingredients

Bara Brith

230g mixed fruit
230g self raising flour
170g dark brown sugar
1 egg
175ml boiling water
2 tea bags

Apple Mixture

4 apples (peeled and diced)
4 tbsp sugar
50ml Gwynt y Ddraig Black Dragon cider
pinch nutmeg
pinch cinnamon
half vanilla pod

Orange Marmalade Ice Cream

8 egg yolks
95g caster sugar
250ml milk
250ml double cream
3 tbsp orange marmalade
zest of 1 orange

Walnut Praline

150g sugar
60ml water
1 tsp glucose
30g walnuts (finely chopped)

Method

For the bara brith

Soak the fruit and tea bags in the boiling water for 15-20 minutes then drain and remove the tea bags. Put the self raising flour and sugar in a mixing bowl and stir in the soaked fruits and the egg until thoroughly combined. Spoon the mixture into a prepared loaf tin. Bake at 160°C for about 45 minutes until well risen and browned. Set aside to cool.

For the apple mixture

Cook all the ingredients together until the apples have softened. Take half the apple and puree it. Set the two apple mixtures aside.

For the orange marmalade ice cream

Whisk the egg yolks, sugar and marmalade together in a bowl. Boil the milk and orange zest and then pour it over the egg mixture. Return the mixture to the pan and heat it until it has thickened, stirring continuously. Pour in the cream and then allow it to cool before churning it in an ice cream maker.

For the walnut praline

Boil the sugar, water and glucose in a pan until golden. Carefully add the walnuts and then pour onto a large sheet of parchment paper. Cover with another piece of paper and roll out the praline until 3mm thin (be careful as it will be very hot). Take off the top layer of parchment and cut out circles of praline. Carefully place these over an oiled ladle and shape into a bowl shape. If the praline hardens, just place it in an oven until soft again. Set aside to cool to serve the ice cream in later.

To make the bara brith apple charlotte

Slice the Bara Brith into 5mm slices and then cut it into rectangles. Brush both sides of the Bara Brith with butter and line a ramekin mould, making sure there are no gaps. Cut a circular piece to line the bottom of the mould. Mix the apple pieces and puree together and spoon them into the centre of the prepared moulds. Cover with a final circle of Bara Brith. Bake at 180°C for about 30 minutes until golden brown.

To serve

Turn out the Charlotte onto the centre of the plate. Place a walnut praline basket next to the Charlotte and scoop some orange marmalade ice cream into the basket. Garnish the ice cream with a slice of dried candied orange.

We like to finish the dish with clotted cream foam and a few sultanas.

140
MAES YR HAF

Parkmill, Swansea SA3 2EH

01792 371 000
www.maes-yr-haf.com

Maes Yr Haf is a five star restaurant with rooms that is recommended by The Good Food Guide, The AA and, more recently, The Michelin Guide. Located in the picturesque village of Parkmill in Gower, and just a short walk from Three Cliffs Bay, there is the Award Winning "Best Beach" which is beloved by all who visit, including local celebrity Catherine Zeta Jones. We are a relatively new establishment which is going from strength to strength each and every year.

The modern, contemporary restaurant is a hot ticket in these parts. Our cuisine is inventive as well as classic with the accent firmly on local Gower produce and modern cooking. The bedrooms, finished in modern muted tones, display the same kind of flair, style, comfort and quality.

Your hosts are General Manager Mark Wicks and Head Chef Ben Griffiths. Along with their team, they are dedicated to making sure your time at Maes Yr Haf is truly memorable.

The modern, contemporary restaurant is a hot ticket in these parts. Our cuisine is inventive as well as classic with the accent firmly on local Gower produce and modern cooking. The bedrooms, finished in modern muted tones, display the same kind of flair, style, comfort and quality

OXWICH POINT LOBSTER RAVIOLI, GOWER SAMPHIRE AND BISQUE EMULSION

SERVES 4

*Leiras - Albariño Rias Baixas 2010
(Spain)*

Ingredients

Ravioli Filling

1 Oxwich Point lobster (cooked)
200g salmon mousse
10g chives and chervil (chopped)

Pasta

200g "OO" pasta flour
2 large free range eggs
2 tbsp olive oil
pinch of salt

Garnish

400ml lobster bisque
400g samphire (washed and picked)
10g tomato concasse
4 sprigs of sea purslane

Lobster Bisque

cracked lobster shell and legs
1 stick celery (chopped)
2 shallots (peeled and sliced)
1 carrot (peeled and chopped)
half bulb fennel (chopped)
bouquet garni
knob of ginger (peeled and sliced)
2 cardamom pods
3 cloves garlic (peeled and sliced)
50ml pernod
50ml brandy
50ml dry vermouth
1tbsp tomato purée
800ml fish stock
75ml olive oil
25ml double cream

Method

Firstly, remove the cooked lobster from its shell, neatly dicing it into small bite-sized nuggets, keeping the shell for the bisque. Fold the lobster nuggets through the salmon mousse and add the chives and chervil. Season lightly, then place into the refrigerator to chill.

For the lobster bisque

Roast the lobster shell and legs in a hot oven for 25 minutes. In a pan, sweat the vegetables, garlic, ginger and bouquet garni, along with the cardamom and olive oil, for 5 – 10 minutes. Add the tomato purée then fry for a further 3 minutes. De-glaze the pan with the Pernod, vermouth and brandy, and reduce down until almost all of the liquid has evaporated.

Add the roasted lobster shell and legs to the pan and stir well, then add the fish stock and bring it to the boil. Lower to a simmering heat and cook for 40 minutes. Pass through a sieve into a clean pan, pressing the stock through with the back of a ladle to extract as much flavour as possible. Reduce a little more and then finish with the cream. Season to taste and keep warm until needed.

For the pasta

Make a well in the flour and crack the eggs into its centre, before adding the salt and olive oil. Work in from the edges and knead until it comes together to form a ball. Refrigerate for a minimum of 30 minutes.

For the ravioli

Bring the pasta dough to room temperature and roll it using a pasta machine on its finest setting. Dust the work surface with flour to prevent the pasta sticking. Cut out eight circles of pasta using a set of 70mm cutters. Place a ball of the lobster and salmon mousse in the centre of four of the circles, and use a little egg yolk around the edges to seal a second circle of pasta on top. Take care to expel all excess air from between the two pasta discs.

To assemble

Cook the ravioli by adding a few drops of olive oil and a pinch of salt to a pan of simmering water and cook for 5-6 minutes. Drain and keep warm until needed.

Blanch the samphire in the same pan of water for 4 minutes and then drain.

Heat the bisque in a pan and foam up using a stick blender.

To serve

Place a neat mound of samphire in the middle of a bowl and top with ravioli. Carefully spoon the emulsified lobster bisque around and garnish the plate with tomato concasse and sea purslane.

A TASTING OF WELSH PEDIGREE PORK, CELERIAC AND APPLE

SERVES 4

🍷 *Ruffino - Aziano Chianti Classico 2008 (Italy)*

Ingredients

1 pork fillet (seasoned, trimmed and rolled in clingfilm)
1 kg belly pork
homemade sausage roll (large)
crackling dust
4 tbsp apple puree, 4 tbsp celeriac puree
150ml taffy apple pork jus
200g shredded Savoy cabbage (blanched and refreshed)
1 bunch baby carrots (blanched)

Black Pudding Beignet

125g blackpudding
salt and white pepper

Potato, Bacon and Onion Terrine

6 Large Maris Piper potatoes
200g cooked bacon off cuts (finely diced)
125g (cooked onion dice)
25g fresh sage (chopped)
300ml melted duck and bacon fat

To make basic tempura batter please see recipe in full on the Relish website

Method

For the belly pork

Slowly confit the belly pork in duck fat for 5 hours at 140°C. Once cooked, press and chill overnight, cut in to four squares and reheat when needed.

For the black pudding beignet

Blend the black pudding and season it lightly. Then quenelle and fry the black pudding in a light tempura batter. Keep warm until needed.

For the potato, bacon and onion terrine

Peel and slice the potatoes on a mandoline. Layer them in a terrine mould with cooked, flaked bacon, onion and sage, pouring over the bacon and duck fat. Season and cook in the oven for two hours at 160°C until the potatoes are cooked. Cool and press using a heavy weight on top of the terrine dish. Leave to set overnight. Cut into portions and warm through when needed.

For the pork fillet

Poach the pork fillet for 8 minutes then colour in a frying pan. Roll in crackling crumbs and heat through in the oven until medium done. Rest in a warm place until needed.

To serve

Heat the sausage roll until browned and cooked through. Reheat the garnishes, cabbage, baby carrots and purées. Warm the taffy apple jus. On a large, oval plate, place a long drag of celeriac purée on one side, then a long drag of apple purée on the other side. Place two mounds of Savoy cabbage onto the plate and top one with a square of the confit belly pork and the other one with pork fillet. Place the potato terrine between them and top with a black pudding beignet. Alongside that, place the homemade sausage roll, garnishing with the baby carrots and the taffy apple jus.

PEANUT PARFAIT, CHOCOLATE CREAM, SALTED CARAMEL

SERVES 6

🍷 *Tokaji Late Harvest Classic Cuvée 2004 (Hungary)*

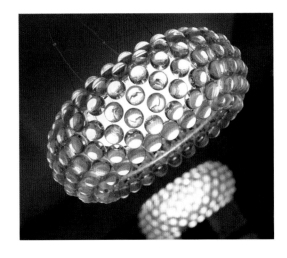

Ingredients

Peanut Parfait

400ml double cream
125g peanut butter
25ml vodka
¼ tin condensed milk

Chocolate Cream

100ml double cream
100ml whole milk
2 egg yolks
100g dark chocolate

To Garnish

caramel sauce
chocolate sauce
chocolate marble
Anglesey sea salt
peanut praline crumble
peanut tuile

Method

For the peanut parfait

Whip the cream until it forms soft peaks. Mix all of the other ingredients together and fold them through the cream. Place into cylinder moulds and freeze.

For the chocolate cream

In a heavy-based pan, slowly heat the milk, cream and egg yolks to 86°C whilst stirring occasionally. Once the mixture has reached 86°C, remove from the heat and fold into the chocolate thoroughly. Refrigerate until needed.

To serve

Dress the plate with swipes and dots of the chocolate and caramel sauce, adding a touch of sea salt to each. Place a rectangle piece of chocolate marble in the centre of each plate. Roll the parfait in the praline crumble and place it on one end of the marble. Next place a quenelle of chocolate cream at the opposite end, and top with the peanut tuile garnish.

150
MANORHAUS

Restaurant-with-Rooms, Well Street, Ruthin, Denbighshire LL15 1AH

01824 704 830
www.manorhaus.com

The Vale of Clwyd in North Wales has many hidden treasures. Manorhaus is one of them; a stylish restaurant-with-rooms in the heart of the historic town of Ruthin and a grade II listed Georgian townhouse. The interiors juxtapose modern design, original features and an array of art. Each of the eight bedrooms - or 'oriel', meaning 'gallery' in Welsh - have interior design inspired by the work of a Welsh contemporary artist. Guest facilities include a cinema, sauna and steam room and a library packed with design tomes, DVDs and guides to the area. The surrounding area is a rich and verdant backdrop that supplies manorhaus with the finest locally sourced, seasonal produce such as Elwy Valley lamb and Welsh Black beef, free-range Ty'n y Celyn chicken and Menai mussels, to name but a few. With a contemporary twist, the menu displays an innovative and creative flair as well as a passion for allowing true flavours to shine. As finalists in the National Tourism Awards for Wales ('Best Place to Stay') and winners of the 'Arts & Small Business Award' 2011, Manorhaus are currently celebrating ten successful years in 2012, and have carved a unique position in the North Wales dining scene. Whether for locals celebrating a special event, or for travellers from further afield, Manorhaus delights all guests with its relaxing ambience, attentive yet unobtrusive service, and the smart yet informal dining experience.

As finalists in the National Tourism Awards for Wales ('Best Place to Stay') and winners of the 'Arts & Small Business Award' 2011, Manorhaus are currently celebrating ten successful years in 2012, and have carved a unique position in the North Wales dining scene

PERL LAS MOUSSE WITH WALNUT BISCUIT

SERVES 4

🍷 *Touraine Sauvignon 2008, France*

Ingredients

Mousse

120g Perl Las Blue or Stilton cheese
187ml milk
65ml double cream
2 gelatine leaves

Pear Purée

2 pears (peeled and cored)
pinch mixed spice
100ml water
100g caster sugar

Red Pepper and Pear Relish

1 red pepper
½ red onion
1 pear
100ml red wine vinegar
100g Demerara sugar

Walnut Biscuit

110g walnuts
55g plain flour
110g soft butter
2 egg whites

Method

For the pear purée

Place the ingredients in a pan and gently simmer for 20-30 minutes until the pears are soft. Allow to cool a little before blending until smooth. Refrigerate until needed.

For the relish

Peel and finely dice the pepper, onion and pear. Combine with the remaining ingredients and cook on a low heat for 25 minutes until tender. Refrigerate until needed.

For the mousse

Crumble the blue cheese into a bowl and allow to soften. Heat the milk in a saucepan and pour over the cheese. Allow to cool a little before blending for a few seconds until combined. Pour back into the saucepan and warm sufficiently to melt the added gelatine. Whisk to dissolve, then strain through a fine sieve into a bowl and refrigerate. In a clean bowl, whisk the cream to soft peaks and then fold into the cheese mixture. Create a base for four ring moulds with clingfilm, then spoon enough mixture into each to the top. Chill to set.

For the biscuit

Preheat the oven to 160°C then mix the walnuts and flour in a blender, pulsing to achieve a fine powder. Whisk the butter then fold in the nut and flour mixture and combine. In a separate bowl, whisk the egg whites until blended but not peaking. Fold half into the nut butter mix, then the remainder. On a greased baking sheet or patisserie sheet, spread the mixture with a spatula to a 3mm thick even layer then, with a cookie cutter (the same diameter as the mousse moulds) make a sequence of imprints. Place the baking sheet in the oven for 20-30 minutes until evenly cooked and medium brown. Remove from the oven and re-cut the circular imprints whilst still hot. Allow the biscuits to cool.

To serve

Spoon a little pear purée on individual serving plates and swirl into a circle. Carefully remove the clingfilm base and run a knife around the inside edge of each mousse mould before easing the mousse out onto the biscuit in the centre of the purée. Top the mousse with a small quenelle of relish and garnish with some finely chopped and dressed salad leaf.

MINT CRUSTED RACK OF WELSH LAMB, POTATO AND AUBERGINE TIAN, PEA PURÉE AND LEMON JUS

SERVES 4

 Coto de Imaz Rioja Reserva 2005 , Spain

Ingredients

Lamb

1 rack of lamb (French trimmed)
6 slices white bread (preferably a couple of days old)
2 handfuls fresh mint
4 tbsp clear honey

Potato and Aubergine Tian

2 large knobs butter
6 white potatoes (peeled and sliced into 5mm-10mm rings)
2 aubergines (sliced into 5mm-10mm rings)
2 pinches cumin

Pea Purée

400g garden peas
75ml double cream
75ml vegetable stock
2 sprigs mint

Lemon Jus

1 pint lamb stock
300ml red wine
2 tbsp redcurrant jelly
juice and zest 1 lemon
2 tbsp plain flour
1 small knob butter

Method

For the lamb

Preheat the oven to 180°C. Either portion the rack or leave whole. Heat a little oil in a large, non-stick frying pan and fry the lamb on all sides to seal, until a bronze colour is achieved. Remove from the pan, allow to cool, and keep the fat remaining in the pan for later. Whilst the lamb is cooling, place the white bread, mint and seasoning in a food processor and blend to make the crust. Using a pastry brush, apply a generous coating of honey onto the lamb then cover with the crust mixture. Place onto a tray in the of the oven for 20 minutes if whole, or 10 minutes if portioned. Leave to rest for 5-10 minutes before serving.

For the tian

Place the butter in a large frying pan over a medium heat. Once heated add the sliced potato and cumin and fry for a couple of minutes either side until golden. Remove, season and place onto a baking tray in the oven. Meanwhile, fry the aubergine in the same pan for a couple of minutes either side until soft and place to one side. Remove the potato from the oven when the centre is soft (after approximately 15 minutes) and allow to cool a little. Next place alternating layers of the potato and aubergine onto the baking tray to form stacks, spoon a little of the butter from the pan over the tops and place to one side to be reheated in the oven for 10 minutes before serving.

For the pea purée

Place the peas, vegetable stock and cream into a saucepan and bring to the boil. Simmer for about 5 minutes then place in a food processor and blend. Pass the mixture through a sieve with the back of a spoon and return to the pan to be seasoned by taste and reheated when needed.

For the lemon jus

Place the red wine in a saucepan and bring to the boil. Reduce to one third of its original volume, add the redcurrant jelly, lemon juice, zest and lamb stock and return to the boil. Once boiling, whisk to ensure that the jelly has dissolved and then remove the stock mixture from the pan. Place the fat from the lamb along with the butter into the saucepan and melt. Add the plain flour and combine to form a paste, ensuring it is not too dry and crumbly. Cook on a low heat for a few minutes, stirring to ensure it does not burn. Next add a small amount of the stock mixture, mixing continuously with a wooden spoon. Keep whisking and adding the stock gradually until a desired consistency is reached. This can be kept warm in the pan until needed.

To serve

Assemble as in the picture.

CHOCOLATE RAVIOLI WITH CACEN GRI

SERVES 4

 Quady Elysium Black Muscat 2009 , California

Ingredients

Chocolate Pasta

2 eggs
5 egg yolks
350g pasta flour
25g cocoa
15g icing sugar
½ tbsp salt
½ tbsp olive oil

Filling

200ml double cream
200g dark chocolate (pellets or small chunks)
2 Welsh cakes (Cacen Gri)
zest 1 orange

Accompaniment

Crème Anglaise

¼ pint milk
¼ pint double cream
3 egg yolks
90g caster sugar
½ vanilla pod

Orange Syrup

1 orange (zest)
150ml fresh orange juice
100ml water
250g caster sugar

Method

For the pasta dough

Combine the ingredients in a mixer with a dough hook until smooth, then leave to rest for 1-2 hours in the fridge.

For the filling

Boil the cream with the orange zest in a saucepan, then add to the chocolate and combine to melt. Refrigerate to set, then crumble in the Welsh cake to bind and refrigerate again.

Use a pasta maker or roller to roll out the dough thinly, then cut into 7cm diameter circles with a cutter. Scoop a small ball of filling onto the centre of half of the pasta circles, brush egg wash around the pasta edge then carefully layer another pasta circle on top, pressing down to expel any air and bind the ravioli edge. Dust with a little pasta flour and refrigerate.

For the orange syrup

Create by combining and boiling all of the ingredients in a saucepan before leaving to cool and thicken.

For the crème anglaise

In a stainless steel bowl stir together, using a wooden spoon, the sugar and yolks until well blended. (Do not let this mixture sit too long or a film will develop on the yolks.) In a small saucepan heat the cream and vanilla just to the boiling point. Remove from heat and whisk a few tablespoons of the cream into the yolk mixture. Then, gradually add the remaining cream, whisking constantly. Heat slowly without boiling until it is thick enough to coat the back of a spoon

To serve

Cook the ravioli (allowing two per person) in a pan of rolling boiling water for approximately 3 minutes until 'al dente', then remove and drain. Serve the pasta in a shallow bowl and dust with cocoa. Drizzle the warm crème Anglaise and orange syrup around the pasta and garnish with chocolate shavings or tuille biscuit.

160
MIMOSA
KITCHEN & BAR

Mermaid Quay, Cardiff Bay CF10 5BZ

029 2049 1900
www.mimosakitchen.co.uk
www.mimosacegin.co.uk

Backed by Welsh actor Ioan Gruffudd, Mimosa's celebrity credentials are well-known. However, this is an establishment that has something to offer beyond the hype. Described by The Sunday Times as 'this year's restaurant for Cardiff' upon its opening in 2006, a winner of the prestigious Penderyn Whisky Award and twice entrants in The Good Food Guide, Mimosa has obviously not escaped the critics' attention either. Located in the heart of Cardiff Bay, the interior has a striking contemporary design (that uses a mixture of wood, leather and slate) and attracts a cosmopolitan mix of diners with its bustling yet relaxed ambience. The restaurant takes its name from the tea-clipper which transported Welsh emigrants in 1865 to Patagonia, Argentina, wine from both countries can be found on the list today. Mimosa serves breakfast from 10am, and à la carte from 12pm until 10pm each day. The contemporary menu (which, along with the restaurant's website, is available in both English and Welsh) is all prepared on site and cooked to order, with great care taken to source locally using seasonal, free-range and Fairtrade ingredients.

The à la carte features favourites such as Caul, Welsh Black Beef, Cockles and Laver bread, and Gower Salt Marsh Lamb as well as a wide selection of vegetarian dishes, whilst the highlight of the specials is invariably the line-caught Fish of the Day.

Located in the heart of Cardiff Bay,
the interior of Mimosa has a striking
contemporary design that uses a
mixture of wood, leather and slate and
it attracts a cosmopolitan mix of diners
with its bustling yet relaxed ambience

PANT-YSGAWN GOATS CHEESE AND ROASTED BUTTERNUT SQUASH SALAD

SERVES 4

 Cave de Ribeauvillé Gewürztraminer, Alsace

Method

Place the diced butternut squash on a baking tray along with the spices, syrup, olive oil and seasoning and mix together thoroughly. Then place into a preheated oven at 180°C and roast until soft. When ready, take them out to allow them to cool just a little.

In a mixing bowl, place the leaves, seeds, berries, goats cheese and seasoning. Gently mix through the still warm butternut squash, including the juices from the baking tray, and serve immediately.

To serve

Assemble as in the picture.

Ingredients

1 butternut squash (peeled, seeds removed and diced)
50ml maple syrup
2g chilli flakes
1g ground cinnamon
5ml olive oil
450g rocket leaves
15 torn basil leaves
100g cranberries (dried)
50g pumpkin seeds
175g Pant-Ysgawn goats cheese
seasoning

BLUE POPPY SEED CHICKEN WITH HONEY ROASTED PARSNIPS AND A PARMESAN CREAM SAUCE

SERVES 4

🍷 *La Cote Flamenco Picpoul de Pinet, France*

Ingredients

4 free range chicken breasts
poppy seeds (enough to coat each breast)
150g parsnips (cut into batons, core removed.
Par boil, then refresh in cold water and drain.)
25g butter
25ml honey
50ml dry white wine
100ml double cream
150g Reggiano parmesan
chives
seasoning

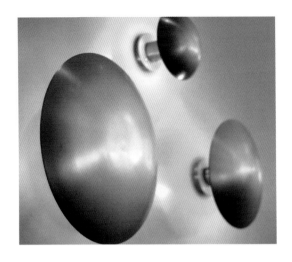

Method

Start by preheating an oven to 200°C.

Coat each chicken breast in the poppy seeds and seasoning. Heat a frying pan with a little olive oil then seal the breast and place it onto a baking tray in the oven.

Whilst the chicken is cooking, use the same frying pan with a little more olive oil and seal off the parsnips to get a little colour, add 25g of the butter and sauté them. Add seasoning and the honey then stir the parsnips well and take them off the heat, placing them on another baking tray in the oven.

For the sauce, heat a saucepan and scald the white wine then add a little seasoning and reduce slightly. Add the double cream and reduce again by half, then lower the heat and add the parmesan. Keep stirring until the sauce is thick.

The chicken breast will now be cooked. If unsure, butterfly it to check. The parsnips should have a golden brown colour by this point also.

To serve

Arrange the parsnips onto a plate in a tidy stack and place the chicken alongside it. Pour the sauce on top and garnish with two chives.

AUTUMN FRUIT JELLY WITH MUSCADEL WINE AND A CARDAMOM AND VANILLA ICE CREAM

SERVES 4

🍷 *Rhona Muscadel Graham Beck, South Africa*

Ingredients

Ice Cream

(makes approximately 600ml)
250ml whole milk
250ml double cream
50g sugar
1 vanilla pod (split)
6 large, free range eggs (yolks)
3 cardamom seeds

Jelly

1 pear (peeled and diced)
1 apple (peeled and diced)
2 plums (peeled and diced)
4 sprigs of thyme
11 gelatine leaves
250g caster sugar
150g ginger (chopped)
8 coriander seeds (crushed)
1 bay leaf
1 green cardamom seed (split into 2)
850ml water
250ml Muscadel wine, or any other dessert wine

Method

For the ice cream

Place the milk, cream, vanilla pod with the seeds and the crushed cardamom into a heavy-based saucepan, then bring to the boil and let it simmer and infuse.

Now mix the sugar and egg yolks together in a large mixing bowl until pale and smooth.

Strain the milk/cream mixture into the egg yolks and sugar, continually whisking whilst you pouring.

Place in an ice cream churner. Alternatively, place into a shallow container in the freezer, giving it a good stir every hour until frozen.

For the jelly

Place the water, wine, thyme, ginger, sugar, coriander seeds, bay leaf and cardamom into a pan and bring to the boil. Allow to simmer for around 90 minutes before passing the mixture through a fine sieve and pouring it back into the same pan.

Poach the fruits in the liquid, starting with the pear and apple as require more poaching time than the plums.

Soak the gelatine leaves in cold water so they are ready when the fruit is poached.

Lift out the fruit, giving a good squeeze to remove any excess water, and stir in the gelatine.

Finally, pour the mixture evenly into four moulds, at the same time dropping in the fruit. The jelly can now be left to set.

To serve

Assemble as in the picture.

170
THE NEWBRIDGE ON USK

Tredunnock, Usk, South Wales NP15 1LY

01633 410 262
www.newbridgeonusk.co.uk

Owned and run by the world-renowned Celtic Manor Resort and situated only a short distance from the resort itself, the Newbridge on Usk is part of the prestigious Celtic Manor collection. Occupying an idyllic location near the picturesque village of Tredunnock, this five star 'restaurant with rooms', with its two AA Rosette award-winning restaurant, provides a relaxing, rural retreat set on the banks of the beautiful River Usk.

Reflecting the setting, the wholesome country fare on offer at The Newbridge is equally award-winning and is lovingly cooked using the finest locally-sourced ingredients, including Usk Valley-reared meat and poultry and venison from the nearby Brecon Beacons. At weekends, guests can enjoy an afternoon of relaxed jazz and swing to accompany one of the best Sunday lunches in the Usk Valley, listening to the sounds of Fats Waller and the legendary Count Basie. A charming 200 year old country inn with a contemporary twist, this quaint and cosy hideaway features rustic fireplaces and wooden floors, and an atmospheric private dining room just off the main restaurant which is the perfect setting to celebrate a special occasion with family or friends.

For those who decide to stay a little longer, six stylish en-suite bedrooms are designed with comfort and elegance in mind, featuring distinctive design, beautiful furnishings, luxurious roll top baths and storm showers.

With its fabulous riverside setting, the Newbridge on Usk also offers guests the opportunity to enjoy some of the best salmon and trout fishing outside of Scotland. An experienced Ghillie will guide you in the skills required to fish this dramatic tidal river and, depending on the season, the restaurant's chefs will prepare and cook your fish so that you can enjoy your own catch for lunch or dinner.

Occupying an idyllic location near the picturesque village of Tredunnock, this five star 'restaurant with rooms', with its two AA Rosette award-winning restaurant, provides a relaxing rural retreat set on the banks of the beautiful River Usk

TEXTURES OF HERITAGE TOMATOES WITH MOZZARELLA AND ROCKET PESTO

SERVES 4

Franschhoek Cellar, Freedom Cross Chenin Blanc, South Africa 2011

Ingredients

Tomato Salad

200g red, yellow and orange heritage tomatoes
200g mozzarella
half a small watermelon
1 small packet wild rocket
1 packet Greek cress
rapeseed oil

Rocket Pesto

50ml rapeseed oil
50g cob nuts
1 clove garlic (peeled)
100g wild rocket
pinch of sea salt

Dried Heritage Tomato Crisps

100g heritage tomatoes (thinly sliced)
200g icing sugar (sifted)

Clear Heritage Tomato Jelly

1.5kg ripe red heritage tomatoes (halved)
2 cloves garlic (blanched in water for 2 minutes)
300ml good quality tomato juice
a few sprigs basil
salt and white pepper
3 gelatine leaves

Method

For the dried heritage tomato crisps

Preheat the oven to 85°C. Lay the finely sliced tomatoes in a single layer on a non-stick baking sheet then dust with the icing sugar. Dry the tomatoes in the oven overnight until they are crisp and candied.

For the clear heritage tomato jelly

Coarsely blend the tomatoes, garlic and basil in a food processor along with some white pepper, salt and 250ml of the tomato juice.

Line a colander with double muslin and place it over a large bowl. Pour the tomato pulp into the colander and leave overnight in the fridge to drain. The next day you should have about 600 - 700ml of clear juice in the bowl.

Soak the gelatine leaves in cold water until soft. Meanwhile, remove a small ladleful of the juice and heat it in a pan. Squeeze the water from the gelatine leaves and stir them into the hot tomato juice until dissolved. Do not boil it. Add the tomato and gelatine to the rest of the juice, along with the remaining 50ml of tomato juice. Stir well and refrigerate for one to two hours until set, then cut into forty 1cm square cubes.

To serve

Place all of the pesto ingredients into a small food processor and blend until smooth. Peel off the watermelon skin then cut out 16 cylinders with an apple corer, trimming the bottoms to ensure all are the same size. Using four plates, start to build the dish in layers. Evenly distribute the watermelon cylinders and allow 50g of mozzarella per person, cut into eight pieces. Drizzle a small amount of rocket pesto over each plate.

Divide the tomato jelly and tomato crisps between the four plates. Slice the raw heritage tomatoes in half and grill 100g of these for 2 minutes. Add a sprinkle of sea salt, then arrange onto the plates with the remaining raw tomatoes, scattering with the Greek cress. Drizzle each plate with a little rapeseed oil and season with ground black pepper and sea salt to serve.

SADDLE OF BRECON VENISON WITH BITTER CHOCOLATE AND BLACKBERRIES

SERVES 4

Châteauneuf-du-Pape, Domaine du Grand Tinel
2006

Ingredients

1 long saddle of venison
6 – 12 thin slices smoked pancetta
50g butter
a few purple potatoes (peeled, boiled and mashed)

Braised Red Cabbage

zest and juice of one orange
6 black peppercorns
1 cinnamon stick
90g Demerara sugar
180g redcurrant jelly
375ml red wine
1 large red cabbage (shredded)

Salsify

6 salsify (peeled and placed in acidulated water to prevent browning)
1 litre chicken stock
1 sprig thyme
3 cloves garlic
6 black peppercorns
3 bay leaves
salt and caster sugar to taste

Poached Blackberries

110g caster sugar
110ml water
150g blackberries

Sauce

100g butter
500g venison bones (reserved from the saddle and chopped by your butcher)
50g onion, 50g carrots (chopped)
12 juniper berries
2 sprigs thyme
2 bay leaves
50g 70% cocoa solids chocolate (finely grated)
50ml crème de mûre (wild blackberry liqueur)

Method

For the braised red cabbage

Place all of the ingredients into a large pan over a medium heat then bring them to the boil. Reduce the heat and simmer gently for two to three hours or until the cabbage is soft and the liquid has reduced in volume to a sauce consistency.

For the venison

Wrap each loin in the smoked pancetta. Heat a frying pan over a medium heat, add the butter and when foaming, add the wrapped venison loins. Fry for 10 - 12 minutes, turning frequently, until the loins are browned all over. Remove from the pan and set aside to rest. Keep warm until ready to serve.

For the salsify

Place the peeled salsify and all of the salsify ingredients into a saucepan and bring to a simmer until just boiling. Reduce the heat and simmer until the salsify are tender (about 12 -15 minutes). Remove the salsify from the pan and set aside.

For the poached blackberries

Place the sugar and water into a saucepan over a medium heat, stirring continuously until the sugar has dissolved and the mixture is just simmering. Add the blackberries and poach gently for two to three minutes or until soft and warm.

For the sauce

Heat a sauté pan until hot then add the butter and venison bones and cook, stirring until the bones are golden brown. Add the carrot, onion, juniper, thyme and bay leaves, stirring occasionally for a further five minutes. Sieve the bones and vegetables into a large saucepan or stockpot, spooning off any excess fat. Pass the sauce through a fine sieve and a double lined muslin cloth into a saucepan and return to the heat. When the sauce has reached the desired consistency, add the chocolate and crème de mûre and stir until the chocolate has melted and the sauce is glossy.

To serve

Place a portion of the red cabbage in the middle of each plate. Carve the venison loin and arrange three pieces of venison per plate on top of the cabbage. Add a portion of the purple potato mash, a few poached blackberries and the salsify, then drizzle the sauce over the venison to finish.

PERRY JELLY AND SUMMER FRUITS WITH ELDERFLOWER ICE CREAM

SERVES 4

Foundstone Raisined Sémillon, Vineyard Premium Selection 2009

Method

For the elderflower ice cream

Bring the milk to the boil in a saucepan and then remove it from the heat. Whisk the egg yolks and sugar together in a bowl, pour in the hot milk and whisk well. Return the mixture to the pan and cook over a low heat for about five minutes, stirring constantly with a whisk so that you do not allow it to boil. Remove from the heat and whisk in the cream and elderflower cordial. Leave to cool then churn in an ice cream machine until thickened. Decant into a clean container and place in the freezer until ready.

For the perry jelly

Immerse the gelatine leaves, one at a time, into a shallow bowl of cold water and leave for a minute or so until soft. Bring 100ml of the perry to the boil in a saucepan, add the sugar and stir until it is dissolved. Drain and squeeze the gelatine leaves and then add them to the hot perry, stirring until melted. Remove from the heat, add the rest of the perry and stir well. Put the pan of jelly somewhere cool, but do not let it set.

To serve

Divide half of the berries into four individual jelly moulds, or use one large mould. Pour in half of the cooled jelly, chill for an hour or so to set, then top up with the rest of the berries and unset jelly. Return them to the fridge to chill until set and then serve with the elderflower ice cream.

Ingredients

Elderflower Ice Cream

300ml whole milk
6 medium, free range egg yolks
100g caster sugar
300ml clotted cream
200ml elderflower cordial

Perry Jelly and Summer Fruits

4 gelatine leaves
500ml perry (sparkling pear cider)
75g caster sugar
125g mixed berries (blueberries, raspberries and wild strawberries)

180
THE OLD RECTORY

Country Hotel & Golf Club, Llangattock, Crickhowell, Powys, Wales NP8 1PH

01873 810 373
www.rectoryhotel.co.uk

D ating back to the end of the 16th century and once the home of Henry Vaughan, Silurist, Breconshire's famous metaphysical poet, The Old Rectory Country Hotel & Golf Club was transformed into a hotel in 1963. The hotel was taken over by Shaun and his team in 2008 and has been completely refurbished to bring it up to 3 star AA standard.

The hotel is situated in Crickhowell, in the heart of the Brecon Beacons and adjoins the Brecon Monmouthshire canal. It provides the perfect location for a weekend away to enjoy the local pursuits of walking, riding, cycling and climbing.

The Old Rectory has 25 bedrooms that range from single rooms to luxurious suites, making it perfect for a couple's weekend away and also for families.

The hotel boasts its own 9 hole, par 3 golf course across fourteen acres amidst fine scenery, with the canal on one side and Crickhowell's majestic Table Mountain on the other.

An orchard forms part of the golf course and also provides autumn fruit to keep the kitchen busy. Surplus apples from their orchard are made into apple juice which is available to purchase in the bar.

The hotel also has an allotment nearby supplying the freshest possible seasonal vegetables to the kitchen.

In addition to the à la carte restaurant and bar, the hotel has a large function room and a smaller conference and private dining room making the hotel a perfect venue for weddings and other special occasions.

The hotel boasts its own 9 hole, par 3 golf course across fourteen acres amidst fine scenery, with the canal on one side and Crickhowell's majestic Table Mountain on the other

GAME TERRINE

SERVES 12

 De Gras Carmenere Reserva, Chile

Ingredients

6 pigeon supremes
4 pheasant supremes
6 red leg partridge supremes
truffle shavings
6 rashers smoked bacon
280ml double cream
pepper

Spiced Pear Chutney

450g onions
6 cloves garlic
3 tbsp olive oil
1.2kg pears (diced)
750g apples (diced)
3 oranges (juice and zest)
6 tbsp ground coriander
3 tbsp turmeric
½ tbsp cayenne
1½ tbsp paprika
1½ tbsp ground ginger
55g butter
125g raisins
150ml red wine vinegar
300g sugar
150g tomatoes (diced)

Garnish

toasted brioche
spiced pear chutney

Method

Blend 2 of the pheasant supremes with cream to make a mousseline. Seal the remaining supremes in a pan.

Line the terrine mould with the smoked bacon. Place layers of the pheasant mousseline and chopped breasts of game. Season and top with truffle shavings.

When filled to the top place the lid on and put in a bain marie in the oven for 30 minutes at 220°C.

For the spiced pear chutney

Sweat down the chopped onions and garlic in olive oil. Add spices and cook out then add butter. Stir in the pears and the apples and cook for 2 minutes. Add the orange juice and zest with raisins and add sugar and vinegar. Reduce until thickened then add the chopped tomatoes for the last two minutes of cooking. Taste and season. Allow to cool then store in sterile jars.

To serve

Plate up the terrine and garnish with the toasted brioche and spiced pear chutney.

LOIN OF LOCAL WELSH LAMB

SERVES 2-4

 Cloudy Bay Pinot Noir

Ingredients

½ loin of Welsh lamb from the saddle
handful of spinach
1 chicken breast
salt and pepper
250ml double cream
pig's caul - crepinette
parsley and rosemary

Potato Rosti

1 Maris Piper potato
2tbsp clarified butter

Sauce

lamb stock
250ml Maderia
1tbsp tomato paste
2tbsp redcurrent jelly
450g root vegetables

Garnish

baby veg and potato rosti

Method

For the lamb

Clean the loin of lamb and seal in a hot pan with olive oil until browned, then season. Make a chicken mousse with the fresh chicken breast and double cream, then add a sprinkle of fresh rosemary and parsley.

Spread the mousse onto the lamb and wrap in blanched spinach and then in the crepinette (or caul fat).

Roast in a non-stick pan for 7 minutes at 230°C.

For the rosti

Use a thin chip mandolin and slice the potato into thin matchsticks. Wash then cook with the clarified butter in a pan, adding a thin layer of the matchstick potatoes each time, making sure each side is golden brown.

For the sauce

Sweat off the root vegetables, add tomato paste, rosemary, redcurrent jelly and Madeira. Then add the lamb stock until the desired thickness is reached. Strain sauce to serve.

To serve

Rest the lamb for 3 minutes then slice. Top with potato rosti and garnish with baby vegetables and lamb sauce.

DUO OF SOUFFLÉS

SERVES 2

🍷 *Brown Brothers Orange Muscat*

Ingredients

This dessert makes 2 soufflés per person, 1 of each flavour

Soufflé

25ml Grand Marnier
4 tbsp crème pâtissière
4 egg whites (whisked)
1 tbsp orange concentrate compound
1 tbsp fresh passion fruit

Orange and Passion Fruit Ice Cream

(makes 1 litre ice cream)
1 litre milk
300g sugar
12 egg yolks
1 tbsp of glucose
250ml cream
orange compound
fresh passion fruit

Method

For the soufflé

Divide 4 tablespoons of crème pâtissière into 2 bowls. Whisk 4 egg whites and divide the mixture into the two bowls. Then add the flavouring orange and Grand Marnier into 1 bowl and passion fruit flavouring into the other.

Spoon the mixtures into 4 buttered and sugared moulds and cook at 270°C in a bain marie for 12 minutes.

For the orange and passion fruit ice cream

Add the milk, sugar, egg yolks, glucose and cream to an ice cream maker.

Then add the flavouring of the orange and passion fruit (for this you must taste as you go along as some fruits are more sour than others). Once this is ready, freeze the mixture.

To serve

Serve 1 of each soufflé with the orange and passion fruit ice cream to finish.

190
PLAS
BODEGROES

Pwllheli. Gwynedd. North Wales LL53 5TH

01758 612 363
www.bodegroes.co.uk

When Chris and Gunna Chown opened Plas Bodegroes in August 1986, the term Restaurant with Rooms was unheard of in Wales, as was any notion of Modern Welsh cookery. Combine this with the geographic remoteness of the property; they chose to achieve their dream, and the dream could easily have become a nightmare. However, their single minded determination was rewarded by becoming the first Welsh restaurant to gain a Michelin-star, followed by three AA-Rosettes and Good Food Guide UK Restaurant of the Year.

Chris and Gunna had a near perfect canvas on which to work. Dreamy, creamy Plas Bodegroes is a Grade 2 Star listed Georgian manor house tucked away in peaceful grounds on the rugged Llyn Peninsula. The locality boasts some of Wales' best walking and beaches, and Chris and Gunna have enhanced the feel of the restaurant with a stunning collection of contemporary Welsh Art, much of it inspired by the Peninsula.

Chris's formula in the kitchen has been a simple one – source the best Welsh ingredients and let them speak for themselves. The results are honest, intense flavours with inventive twists that are well-informed, not faddy. So he uses wind dried Carmarthen ham to enhance his monkfish salad, Glasfryn Parc Welsh Black beef in two ways to reinterpret the classic flavour of beef and onions, and rhubarb and elderflower from his own kitchen garden.

Chris's formula in the kitchen has been a simple one – source the best Welsh ingredients and let them speak for themselves. The results are honest, intense flavours with inventive twists that are well-informed, not faddy

WARM SALAD OF MONKFISH, CARMARTHEN HAM AND MUSHROOMS

SERVES 6

 Tokay Pinot Gris Grand Cru Heimbourg, Zind-Humbrecht 2009

Method

Cut about 50g off the monkfish, and chop this finely. Chop one of the slices of ham finely, and sweat this in olive oil with the chopped monkfish, onion, garlic and broken up mushrooms in a sauteuse, adding a generous amount of ground black pepper but no salt.

Cut the remaining monkfish into 6 even sized slices. Season these well with pepper then chargrill on one side only for a couple of minutes. Add these to the pan, placing them chargrilled side up onto the onion mixture, and add the white wine and vinaigrette.

Cover the pan, and remove from the direct heat but keep warm so the ingredients continue to infuse gently.

Arrange the salad leaves in the centre of 6 plates. Tear each slice of ham into 3 smaller slices, and sear these very quickly on the chargrill or hotplate.

To serve

Arrange three pieces of ham around the salad on each plate then place some of the onion mix onto each salad. Top with the monkfish and dress with the pan juices.

Ingredients

300g monkfish tail (off the bone and trimmed)
7 thin slices Carmarthen ham (about 120g)
12 button mushrooms (broken into coarse pieces)
30g onion (chopped)
1 clove garlic (chopped)
olive oil
50ml white wine
100ml vinaigrette
black pepper
salad leaves including parsley, chervil and rocket

CHARGRILLED SIRLOIN OF GLASFRYN PARC WELSH BLACK BEEF WITH OXTAIL FONDANT

SERVES 6

 Torbreck "The Steading", Barossa 2001

Ingredients

720g eye of sirloin
18 shallots
80g butter
6 potatoes each around 200g
250ml light beef stock
3 thyme sprigs
3 cloves garlic (crushed)
100ml sherry vinegar

1 oxtail (cut into vertebrae by your butcher)
20g plain flour
2 onions (peeled and chopped coarse)
3 carrots (peeled and cut into 1" lengths)
4 bay leaves
150ml port
1 bottle red wine
3 slivers of orange peel
a little olive oil
seasoning

Method

Prepare the shallots first. Roast them in a hot oven for 15 minutes or so; allow to cool then peel them and put aside. Keep the peel to put in with the oxtail bones later.

Prepare the oxtail

Take a pan that will fit in your oven, but is big enough to take all the oxtail pieces in one layer.

Season the oxtail pieces and coat them with flour. Heat the olive oil in the pan, brown the oxtail in the olive oil, then add all the other ingredients. The wine should just about cover the meat, but top with a little water if it doesn't. Cover the pan, and cook at 120°C in the oven for 5 hours (you can also do this on a bare simmer on the hot top).

After 5 hours, remove the pan from the oven and allow to cool for a few minutes or until you can touch it. Strain the whole caboodle over another pan.

Remove the meat from the bones. The meat shouldn't fall off, but should pull off easily. If it doesn't put it back for two hours. Keep the meat and carrots on one side.

Place the bones and retained shallot skins back into the juice in the pan, and boil for another hour.

Strain this onto your retained oxtail meat.

For the potatoes

Cut each into a drum 2" tall and 2" in diameter. Hollow out the top of the drum to make a container.

Fry the potatoes top and bottom in butter in a sauteuse. Add the beef stock to almost cover. Add thyme and garlic, and then simmer the potatoes until they have absorbed some of the stock and are cooked.

Place the shallots in another pan with the sherry vinegar and the last 50g of butter. Sweat until the vinegar has evaporated and allow the shallots to fry until browned. Add 100 ml of the oxtail gravy and reduce to a sticky glaze. Remove the shallots, keep warm, and add the oxtail to the pan to reheat it all.

Cut the sirloin into 6 equal sized thick rounds. Season well and chargrill these to your liking.

To serve

Place a potato onto each of the 6 plates. Spoon some oxtail into each potato. Surround with carved sirloin, some retained carrots and 3 shallots each and coat with the oxtail gravy.

CINNAMON BISCUIT OF APPLE AND RHUBARB WITH ELDERFLOWER CUSTARD

SERVES 6

🍷 *Château Lafaurie Peyraguey 1988*

Ingredients

Pastry

200g plain flour
60g ground almonds
90g icing sugar
large pinch ground cloves
1 tsp ground cinnamon
120g butter (diced small but kept cold)
1 egg yolk
splash milk
caster sugar

Compote and Sorbet

400g pink rhubarb
400g Bramley apples
150g caster sugar
1 vanilla pod
30ml elderflower cordial
150g whipped cream

Custard

4 egg yolks
40g caster sugar
100ml cream
150ml milk
50ml elderflower cordial

Method

For the pastry

Combine all of the pastry ingredients in a food processor, keeping them as cold as possible. Bring together and allow the mixture to rest for at least 2 hours.

Roll the pastry out quickly on a floured cold surface. It should be very thin. It will be difficult to work with. Cut into 12 heart shapes, lay on a baking sheet and sprinkle lightly with caster sugar. Allow to rest in the fridge for at least an hour and then bake at 160°C for about 8 minutes until the biscuits are mid brown and crisp. Cool on a wire rack. When cool, they will keep in an airtight container for a few days.

For the compote and sorbet

Peel, core and chop the apples. Peel the rhubarb, retain only the bottom 10" or so, and cut into 1" pieces. Place these into a pan with the sugar, cordial and vanilla. Cover and stew gently until the fruit is soft but not mushy. Remove from the pan and strain, retaining the strained juice. Cool this juice and churn in an ice cream machine for the sorbet.

For the custard

Scald the milk and cream together. Whisk this into the egg yolks and sugar. Heat the custard to thicken and add the elderflower cordial. Allow to cool.

To serve

"Butter" the topside of one biscuit and the underside of another with a little whipped cream and fill with the compote like a sandwich. Surround with custard and add a scoop of the sorbet.

200
THE QUEEN'S HEAD

Glanwydden, Conwy LL31 9JP

01492 546 570
www.queensheadglanwydden.co.uk

The village of Glanwydden is just five minutes drive from the Victorian seaside resort of Llandudno, with its shops and grand, curving beach. In the other direction lies the countryside and Snowdonia National Park, making this 18th century pub and restaurant ideally placed for both.

One of the finest and best-known inns in Wales, one that is listed in all of the major food guides and which attracts food lovers from far and wide, this old wheelwright's cottage has certainly gone up in the world. Now there are low beams, polished tables, walls strewn with maps and a roaring log fire in the bar. Professional chefs who have a passion for local produce prepare and present an impressive range of delicious dishes that in the summer might include fresh Conwy crab and Great Orme lobster. A friendly, smartly turned-out staff serve starters of crispy duck leg or Conwy fish soup, and mains of salmon and coriander fishcakes or Welsh rump steak with garlic butter. Desserts might include brioche bread and butter pudding. An impressive selection of wines and beers are also available which can be taken out on the pretty terrace on a hot summer's day.

Robert and Sally Cureton have been here for 29 years, nurturing a country local, and their efforts paid off when they were awarded AA's Pub of the Year for Wales 2009-2010.

Complete the treat by booking a stay in the Old Parish Storehouse across the road, a sweet retreat for two that ensures a comfortable and decadent stay.

Professional chefs who have a passion for local produce prepare and present an impressive range of delicious dishes that in the summer might include fresh Conwy crab and Great Orme lobster

LOCAL SMOKED SALMON WITH A LEMON & DILL PANNA COTTA

SERVES 6

Los Gansos Gewürztraminer, Chile

Method

Put 6 small pudding moulds (about 120 ml each) onto a baking tray.

Soak the gelatine leaves in a bowl of very cold water and set aside.

Add the cream and milk into a heavy-bottomed pan and bring it slowly to the boil. When the cream is boiling, add the lemon juice and zest and whisk together thoroughly. Simmer for a few minutes so that the liquid reduces slightly and then turn off the heat.

Remove the softened gelatine and squeeze out any excess water. Stir the gelatine into the hot cream and set aside until just warm. Strain the cream into a jug and add the chopped dill. Place in the fridge, whisking for a few minutes until slightly set. Finally, pour the slightly set cream into the pudding moulds and place in fridge for 5 hours.

To serve

Remove the panna cotta from its mould onto the middle of a plate. Arrange smoked salmon around the panna cotta and finish with capers and lemon.

Ingredients

450g Llandudno smoked salmon

600ml double cream
150ml semi skimmed milk
zest of one lemon
squeeze of lemon juice
3 leaves gelatine
1 heaped tbsp fresh dill
salt and pepper

POT ROASTED ANGLESEY PARTRIDGE WITH BRAISED PUY LENTILS AND RED CABBAGE

SERVES 4

🍷 *Château Lamothe 1er Côtes de Bordeaux, France*

Ingredients

Pot Roasted Anglesey Partridge

4 partridge
4 rashers pancetta
1 onion
2 carrots
2 parsnips
1 sprig thyme
2 bay leaves
1tsp redcurrant jelly
570ml chicken stock
salt and black pepper
70ml port wine
2tbsp sunflower oil
55g Welsh butter

Braised Puy Lentils and Red Cabbage

3 tbsp sunflower oil
1 large onion (thinly sliced)
2 garlic cloves (crushed)
340g puy lentils
500g red cabbage
2 sweet apples
1 litre chicken stock
Welsh honey
salt and black pepper

Method

For the partridge

Season each partridge really well then heat the oil in a casserole dish and add the partridge. Spend about 10 minutes making sure the meat is well coloured on all sides, using the tongs to turn them when needed.

Remove the meat from the dish and add a splash more oil. Add all the vegetables, thyme and bay leaves. Position the birds on top of the vegetables, pour over the chicken stock and add the pancetta on top of the birds. Place the dish into the oven, uncovered, for 35-45 minutes at 190°C.

Remove the dish from the oven, lift out the birds and pancetta and set them aside to rest. Meanwhile, sieve the cooking liquor and skim off any fat. Add a little port wine and redcurrant jelly then bring it to the boil, whisking in some butter to thicken it. Season with salt and black pepper.

For the braised puy lentils and red cabbage

Heat the oil in a saucepan and fry the onion over a medium heat for three minutes while stirring occasionally. Add the garlic and fry for a further minute.

Add the lentils and stir for 3 minutes or until they have absorbed the oil.

Pour in the chicken stock then cover and place it in the oven for 20 minutes. Remove the pan from the oven and add the diced red cabbage, apples and honey. Cook for a further 20 minutes until the ingredients are soft. Taste and season as desired.

To serve

Place a partridge and some of the pancetta on top of the puy lentils and red cabbage. Drizzle over the port wine sauce. Further accompaniments to this dish can be game chips and bread sauce.

PAVLOVA

SERVES 6

🍷 *Château Manos, Cadillac, France*

Ingredients

3 fresh, large egg whites
170g caster sugar
1tsp raspberry vinegar
1tsp cornflour

Topping

300ml whipping cream
340g raspberries and blueberries

Coulis

250g strawberries
50g caster sugar
1tsp lemon juice

Method

Pre heat the oven to 150°C.

Place the egg whites into a large clean bowl and have the sugar measured and ready. Now whisk the egg whites until they form soft peaks and you can turn the bowl upside-down without them sliding out.

Start to whisk in the sugar, approximately 30g at a time, whisking after each addition, until all the sugar is in. Spoon the meringue mixture into a piping bag and pipe out 6 circles onto a lined baking tray. Start in the centre and work out. Place the baking tray in the oven, turning down the heat to 140°C and leave to cook for one hour.

Turn the heat off but leave the Pavlova inside the oven until it is completely cold.

For the strawberry coulis

Wash, dry and hull the strawberries then place them in a food processor with sugar and lemon juice. Blend them together until the sauce is glossy and the sugar has dissolved.

Pour the sauce through a fine sieve, pushing it through and mixing with the back of a wooden spoon. Taste for sweetness and adjust the sugar accordingly.

To serve

Lift the pavlova off the baking sheet and place it on a serving dish. Just before serving, spread the whipped cream on top, arrange the fruit on top of the cream and drizzle the fruit coulis. Dust with a little sifted icing sugar.

210
SEAVIEW RESTAURANT WITH ROOMS

Market Lane, Laugharne, Carmarthen, Dyfed SA33 4SB

01994 427 030
www.seaview-laugharne.co.uk

The aspiration when this building was bought in the July of 2007, was to restore the derelict neglected building back to the former glory of this Georgian fronted building. With painstaking restoration this has been achieved and now the former home of world famous poet Dylan Thomas is protected for generations to come. The rooms are exquisite and charming, yet humble and simple. They all enjoy sea views and are finished to the highest quality. Seaview is located in the old part of Laugharne, and it takes its place in the heritage of this township yet remains tranquil and private.

Seaview has a creative history with poet Dylan Thomas having previously lived and worked here. This creativity has now been continued with Darren Jory taking the helm, not at the writing desk but rather on his creative platform, the kitchen. Seaview has one clear aspiration and that is that the food they serve is simply the best. The emphasis of Seaview is all about the experience, with limited covers in the restaurant and the tables being allocated to customers all evening. The no rush dining experience with interactive time from the chef and the staff creates a real dining experience. A must is the tasting menu, a true culinary experience which has been developed using all local wares and embrace in the unique area in which Seaview is located.

Seaview is very much a destination restaurant with rooms, a night here with dinner is a must, it is quite simply romantic and relaxing and it offers a truly unique dining experience of the highest quality.

Seaview has a creative history with poet Dylan Thomas having previously lived and worked here. This creativity has now been continued with Darren Jory taking the helm, not at the writing desk but rather on his creative platform, the kitchen

WILD GROUSE, CARMARTHEN HAM, PONT GAR BLUE AND PEAR

SERVES 6

Bird in Hand, Two in the Bush. Merlot/Cabernet, Mt Lofty Ranges 2007 Australia

Ingredients

3 wild grouse
6 slices Carmarthen ham
200g Pont Gar blue cheese
100ml double cream
50ml hazelnut oil
2 pears
100ml white balsamic
200ml cider
12 juniper berries
1 sprig rosemary
100ml olive oil
2 small butchers black puddings
ruby chard
celery leaves
sea salt
orange zest
250ml duck fat

Method

For the wild grouse

Prepare the Wild Grouse by removing the breasts and legs. You will need one breast and one leg per person. You could always ask your butcher to do this. Put the breasts in the fridge until needed. Grind 50g of sea salt with the zest of one orange and a pinch of rosemary until well mixed. Rub the mixture into the grouse legs and refrigerate for about 30 minutes. Wash off under cold water and pat dry on a kitchen cloth. Place in an oven dish and cover with the duck fat and cook in the oven at 100°C for 45 minutes or until the legs are giving.

For the pont gar blue

Warm the double cream through, being careful not to boil. Crumble the Pont Gar into the cream and allow to melt while mixing gently. When melted, allow to cool slightly. Transfer to a kitchen blender and blend on a high speed while slowly adding the hazelnut oil. When combined, season with sea salt and black pepper. Set aside in a bowl covered with clingfilm at room temperature.

For the pear

Peel the pears. Bring the balsamic, cider, sugar and four juniper berries to the boil. Add the pears and simmer gently for 20 minutes, then remove from the heat and allow to cool in the liquid.

Slice the black pudding into 1cm discs.

Crush the 8 juniper berries and lightly heat them in a dry pan to release their aroma. Season with a little salt then add the 100ml of olive oil and heat to 70°C. Remove from the heat and cover until cool.

To serve

Pan-fry the wild grouse breasts with the black pudding discs in a heavy-bottom pan with a little olive oil. Re-heat the grouse legs in the oven until crispy. Cut the pear into strips. Place 3 teaspoons of the blue cheese on a warm plate. Place the pear around and the black pudding. Cut the breast into two and season with salt and pepper. Place it on the plate along with the crispy leg. Spread the Carmarthen ham and dress with the juniper oil, celery leaves and ruby chard.

TEFIFI VALLEY SALMON CURED AND GRILLED, CARROT, ORANGE, PICKLED RAISIN, CAPER AND CURRY

SERVES 6

Pouilly-Fumé, Domaine Thibault, André Dezat
2009 France

Ingredients

6 x 180g portions Loch Duart salmon
5 carrots
3 oranges
3 English radish
100g large raisins
100g caper berries
50ml balsamic
30g caster sugar
10g Madras curry powder
50ml grape seed oil
50ml extra virgin olive oil
1 lemon
sea salt
seasonal wild herbs

Method

Cut each portion of salmon into 2 pieces. Place 6 pieces in the fridge until needed. Dice the other 6 pieces into 1 cm dice, place in the fridge until needed.

For the carrots

Peel the 5 carrots. Chop 4 into equal pieces reserve the last until needed. Place the 4 chopped carrots into a pot and cover with water, a little salt and the juice of 1 orange. Bring to the boil and simmer until soft, add more water if needed. When cooked, blend until smooth in an upright blender.

For the raisins

Place the raisins into a bowl with the balsamic and sugar. Pour over 100ml of boiling water and cover the bowl in clingfilm to allow the raisins to absorb the liquid. When cool place in the fridge to chill.

Slice the carrots and radishes wafer thin on a mandolin. Keep them separate in two bowls.

Segment the remaining oranges.

For the salmon

In a dry pan, warm the curry spices through to release their aroma. Season lightly and cover with the grape seed and olive oil. Bring to 70°C then remove from heat and cover until cool.

Place the diced salmon and sliced carrot in the same bowl, season with sea salt, ½ a lemon juiced and ½ an orange juiced mix well and allow to marinade for 5 minutes.

To serve

Place the 6 salmon pieces on to a well oiled tray and grill gently until cooked, season with lemon juice, curry oil and sea salt. Place 3 spoons of the carrot puree on the plate then place the cured salmon, pickled raisin, caper, the rolled cured carrot and the orange segments around the plate. Add the grilled salmon, sliced radish and wild herbs to finish.

DARK CHOCOLATE GANACHE, BEETROOT, RASPBERRY, YOGHURT AND APPLE

SERVES 6

Brown Brothers Orange Muscat, Victoria, 2009 Australia

Method

For the chocolate ganache

Place the chocolate, cream, sugar and glucose syrup in a heat-proof bowl over a pot of simmering water and melt together. Stir occasionally to combine. Remove from the heat and transfer to a plastic container and cool to setting point.

For the beetroot raspberry

In an upright blender, purée 4 of the cooked beetroots with a third of the raspberries and the balsamic until smooth. Season with a little sea salt to finish.

For the yoghurt and apple

Quarter the apples and deseed them. Place in a plastic bowl and freeze. When frozen, place into a kitchen blender and blend with sugar syrup and 1 tsp of sorbet stabiliser.

Churn in an ice cream machine according to the machines specifications.

Mix the yoghurt, whiskey, honey and chopped rosemary together.

To serve

Thinly slice the remaining cooked beetroot on a mandolin.

Spoon two dollops of Ganache on to the plate and garnish with the rest off the ingredients and the remaining raspberries.

Ingredients

Chocolate Ganache

500g dark chocolate
250ml double cream
65g caster sugar
65g glucose syrup
6 small cooked beetroots
I packet English raspberries
20ml aged balsamic
5 Granny Smith apples
150ml sugar syrup
1 tsp sorbet stabiliser
100ml natural yoghurt
20ml Penderyn whiskey
50ml clear honey
1 sprig rosemary (chopped)
pinch Maldon sea salt

220
SOSBAN

North Dock, Llanelli, Carmarthenshire SA15 2LF

01554 270 020
www.sosbanrestaurant.com

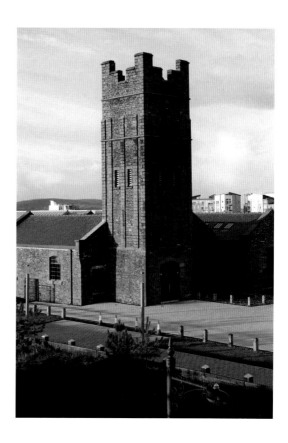

Sosban (Welsh for saucepan!) is located in a magnificent Grade 2 listed building that once provided the neighbouring dock with hydraulic power. Two Welsh Rugby Internationals, Stephen Jones and Dwayne Peel, founded Sosban. They combined forces with food journalist Simon Wright and local construction entrepreneur Robert Williams to redevelop the derelict building into a one hundred cover restaurant serving French bistro style food based on Welsh ingredients.

The building makes the most of its heritage, dominated by stone walls, oak trusses and some dramatic chandeliers designed by a local artist, and the impressive copper-topped bar, formed from an enormous iron water tank, that formed part of the original structure.

The Head chef is Sian Rees, a local girl who left for London at an early stage and rose through the kitchens of Terence Conran and with the Galvin brothers to become Head Chef at the renowned Galvin Bistrot de Luxe in Baker Street. The cooking is unfussy and classic but refined. Their signature dishes on the menu may include a starter dish of crab lasagne or a main course like pithiver of wood pigeon. There is a well-thought out and fairly priced wine list complemented by a neat selection of craft beers and a regularly changing cocktail list.

The building makes the most of its heritage, dominated by stone walls, oak trusses and some dramatic chandeliers designed by a local artist with the impressive copper-topped bar, formed from an enormous iron water tank, that formed part of the original structure

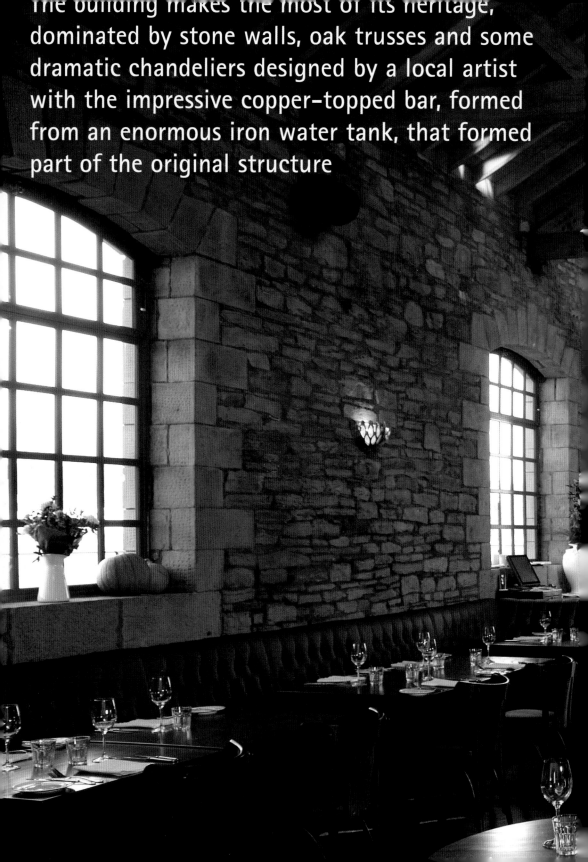

CHICKEN, HAM HOCK AND FOIE GRAS TERRINE

SERVES 12

🍷 *Muscadet Sur Lie Côtes de Grandlieu 2009 (France)*

Ingredients

Terrine

4 chicken breasts (cooked)
1 ham hock (to cook the ham hock: you need 1 carrot, 1 onion, 1 leek, bay leaf, 1 stick of celery)
100g grade A foie gras
100g wild mushrooms
100g peeled button onions
2 leeks
4 leaves of golden gelatine (soaked in cold water)
salt and pepper
1 x 2 litre terrine mould

Gribiche Sauce

150g mayonnaise
50g capers (finely chopped)
50g cornichons (finely chopped)
1 hard boiled egg (finely chopped, yolk and white separately)
tarragon, parsley and chervil (finely chopped)

To serve

25g mixed leaf salad
olive oil
lemon

Method

For the terrine

Pre heat an oven to 120°C. Place the ham hock in a pan large enough to take the hock and all of the vegetables. Cover with water, bring to the boil on the stove and place in the oven for 3 hours or until the ham hock is cooked (the bone should pull out easily once cooked). Leave to cool in the stock.

Cut the leeks in half, wash and cook in a pan of boiling, salted water for 4 minutes. Refresh in a bowl of iced water to prevent them from cooking further. Drain and leave to one side.

Sauté the wild mushrooms in some butter until cooked and then reserve to one side for later.

Cook the button onions in a pan with a little butter and some of the ham stock (enough to cover the onions). Place into a hot oven for about 8-10 minutes. Drain and add to the mushrooms.

Remove the ham hock from the stock, pass the stock through muslin and return to the heat. Reduce the stock until the flavour is concentrated but the stock is not too salty. Measure 1 litre of stock, add the gelatine and whisk until the gelatine is dissolved.

Pull the meat from the ham hock, discard the fat and bone, and add the meat to the onions and mushrooms. Season to taste.

Line the terrine mould with a double layer of clingfilm.

Line the terrine mould with the leeks, overlapping each strip ¼ over the next along both sides until the mould is covered.

Sear the foie gras in a hot pan until cooked (2-3 minutes).

Cut the cooked chicken breasts into four even strips.

Place some of the ham, mushroom and onion mix into the mould. Next add some of the chicken, and then cover with more ham and mushroom until the terrine is half full. Then layer the cooked foie gras in the middle of the terrine. Fill the terrine with the rest of the chicken, ham and mushroom mix. Once the terrine is full, pour over the reduced ham stock to cover. Arrange the remaining leeks to cover the terrine on top. Cover with clingfilm and refrigerate for 24 hours before using

For the gribiche sauce

Mix all of the ingredients with the mayonnaise and season to taste.

To serve

Remove the terrine from the mould and cut into 1cm slices, then plate. Add a quenelle of gribiche sauce and a little salad dressed with some olive oil and lemon juice.

BRAISED AND ROASTED GOWER SALT MARSH LAMB

SERVES 4

 Côtes du Ventoux Grandes Serres Rhone 2009 (France)

Ingredients

Lamb

1 loin of Gower salt marsh lamb
1 belly of Gower salt marsh lamb (1 carrot, 1 onion, 1 celery, 1 bay leaf, sprig of thyme, 1 clove garlic, 1 leek, 100ml red wine)
1 French-trimmed rack of Gower salt marsh lamb

Carrot Purée

8 medium carrots (peeled and finely chopped)
80g butter
salt and pepper

Sauce

100ml red wine
The cooking liquor from the lamb belly
100g shallots (peeled and sliced)
100g carrots (peeled and chopped)

To Serve

50g peeled button onions (cooked)
12 baby carrots (cooked)
4 baby turnips (cooked)
12 new potatoes (peeled)
200g baby spinach (washed and lightly sautéed)

Method

For the lamb belly

Preheat your oven to 120°C.

Seal the lamb belly in a pan (large enough to accommodate both the lamb and the vegetables). Remove the lamb and reserve to one side. In the same pan, sweat down the vegetables, add the red wine then reduce. Return the lamb to the pan, cover with water and bring this to the boil. Place into the oven for 3-4 hours or until the lamb belly is cooked tender. Allow to cool in the stock.

Once cool, remove the lamb belly from the stock, pull off any excess fat or bones and roll the lamb belly in some clingfilm, reserving the cooking liquor for the sauce. Refrigerate for 2-3 hours or until set.

Pass the cooking liquor and reserve the lamb belly stock.

For the sauce

Sweat the shallots and carrots in a pan, add the red wine and reduce to almost nothing.

Add the lamb belly stock and bring this to the boil. Skim off any fat and simmer this to a sauce consistency, skimming all the time.

Season to taste, pass and reserve to one side.

For the carrot purée

Melt the butter in a pan, add the carrots and cover until cooked. Once cooked, blend until smooth and season to taste.

Set aside.

Preheat your oven to 200°C.

Season the lamb rack and loin, and in a hot pan seal both. Cook in the oven for 9 minutes before leaving to rest for 4 minutes. Slice the lamb belly into four pieces and seal in a hot pan on both sides. Heat in the oven for 3-4 minutes whilst the rack and loin are resting. Next, cut the lamb rack and loin into four pieces each.

To serve

Place the spinach in the middle of the plate, placing one piece of belly, one piece of rack and one piece of loin on each plate on top of the spinach. Add one spoon of carrot purée, as well as the vegetables and potatoes to each plate. Pour over some sauce and serve immediately.

TART TATIN

SERVES 4

🍷 *Sauternes Clos l'Abeilley 2005*
   (France)

Method

Preheat your oven to 200°C. Peel the apples, cut them in half and remove the core. Butter the base of each of the four 4 inch diameter pans using 25g of butter in each. Then sprinkle 3 dessert spoons of caster sugar on top the butter in each pan.

Place 3 halves of apple into each pan and cover with the puff pastry. Making a small hole in the top of each one. Place your tart tatins in the oven for 35-40 minutes or until the apples are cooked and caramelized.

To serve

Turn the tart tatins out of the pan onto a plate and accompany them with vanilla ice cream and a glass of Sauternes Clos l'Abeilley.

Ingredients

12 Braeburn apples
12 dsp of caster sugar
100g unsalted butter
4 puff pastry discs
4 scoops of vanilla ice cream

230
THREE SALMONS HOTEL

Bridge Street, Usk, Monmouthshire NP15 1RY

01291 672 133
www.threesalmons.co.uk

The Three Salmons Hotel is nestled in the centre of the idyllic Welsh market town of Usk. Dating back 300 years, the property has always been synonymous with hospitality and good food. Purchased by its current owners in 2010, the property has witnessed an extensive renovation programme which has seen a complete refurbishment of its function suites, bedrooms and dining room, but remaining sympathetic to the history and heritage of the property. The hotel is the ideal base to explore the Brecon Beacons, or fish the world famous River Usk or The River Wye, and after a day in the great outdoors there is nothing quite like retiring back to the hotel to sample the genuine hospitality and an award-winning dinner. Since opening in January 2010, James Bumpass has taken the role of head chef and has earned two well deserved AA Rosettes for his cooking within the first 18 months. His career to date has seen him work with the likes of John Campbell within the Sir Peter Michael collection, as well as overseeing the food for the Welsh Rugby Union at The Vale Resort. Using the finest local commodities from our doorstep, including Usk Valley beef and vegetables grown in our own garden, his food is modern British and well executed, which has earned deserved praise from both the industry and our patrons. To complement his food there is an ever-changing wine list plus a selection of real ales and ciders from the local area.

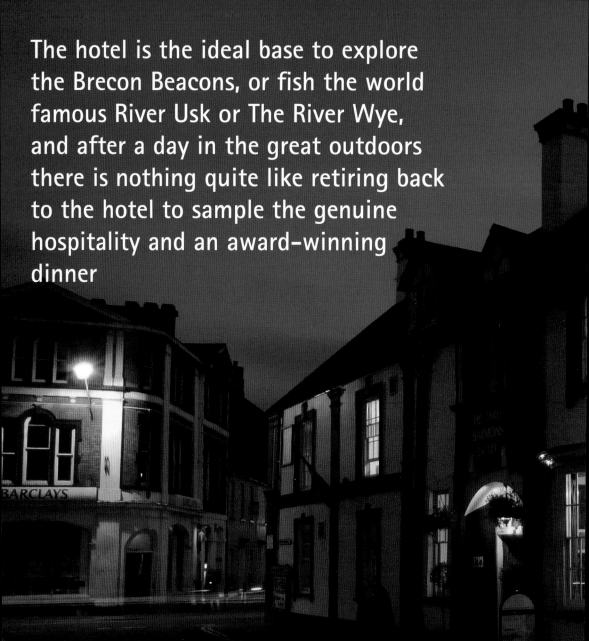

The hotel is the ideal base to explore the Brecon Beacons, or fish the world famous River Usk or The River Wye, and after a day in the great outdoors there is nothing quite like retiring back to the hotel to sample the genuine hospitality and an award-winning dinner

CRAB BISQUE CANNELLONI, SWEETCORN PURÉE

SERVES 4

Touraine Sauvignon Blanc, Les Nuages, Loire 2010

Ingredients

Bisque Jelly

1 kg crab bones
1 star anise
80g shallots (chopped)
5g chervil
3g thyme
2 cloves garlic
70g tomato purée
80g sliced white leek
150ml white wine
50ml brandy
1.2 litres chicken stock
2.5g agar agar
dash of cooking oil

Filling

240g picked white crab meat
50g cucumber (peeled finely diced)
80g good mayonnaise
seasoning

Sweetcorn Purée

150g sweetcorn
15g butter
100ml milk
100ml cream

Method

For the bisque jelly

Fry crab bones hard to release the flavour. Add tomato purée. Add all the vegetables and herbs then add brandy, white wine and chicken stock all in quick succession.

Simmer for one hour. Pass through a sieve and yield approximately 500ml. Reduce to 200ml and then add agar and bring to the boil to activate. Pour onto a large square plate and allow to cool in the refrigerator for 2 hours. Once cooled cut into rectangles.

For the filling

Combine all ingredients and divide into four. Place on jelly rectangles and roll into a barrel.

For the sweetcorn purée

Simmer all together until the liquid begins to thicken. Liquidise and pass through a sieve. Serve when it is still warm.

To serve

Assemble as in the picture. Garnish with rocket and five chick peas.

LOIN OF VENISON, CELERIAC & CARROT POTATO CAKE, RED CABBAGE

SERVES 4

 Vondeling Erica Shiraz, South Africa.
2007

Ingredients

Venison

800g Welsh venison loin (cleaned and trimmed)
½ bulb of garlic
6g thyme
125g butter
dash of cooking oil

Red Cabbage

300g red cabbage (sliced 3mm thick)
250ml red wine
180g sugar
75g redcurrant jelly
1g all spice

Celeriac and Carrot, Potato Cake

1.2kg potato (thinly sliced)
100g celeriac (thinly sliced)
60g carrot (thinly sliced length ways)
200ml cream
20g garlic (crushed)

Carrot Swipe

100g carrots
100ml milk
200ml double cream
55g butter

Method

For the venison

Heat a heavy bottomed pan and add oil. Add venison, thyme and garlic ensuring to colour venison on all sides. Add the butter and when the butter starts to foam; baste the venison turning regularly.

Continue until the venison begins to firm up, then remove from heat and allow to rest in the pan for 5-7 minutes. Carve and serve.

For the red cabbage

Add all the ingredients to a heavy bottomed pan and reduce until the liquid has become sticky.

For the celeriac and carrot, potato cake

Boil the cream and pour over the sliced vegetables. Layer alternately in a cast iron stew pot.

Cover with baking paper and foil at 180°C for about 2 hours.

Press and chill and then turn out. Portion and place back in the oven for 18 minutes 180°C.

For the carrot swipe

Chop the carrots and simmer in butter until the butter turns orange. Add all the liquid ingredients and simmer until the sauce begins to thicken. Puree and use whilst warm.

To serve

Assemble as in the dish.

TREACLE TART, TOFFEE SAUCE, CLOTTED CREAM

SERVES 4

Banyuls, Domaine de la Rectorie, Roussillon. 2007

Method

For the treacle tart base

Cream the butter and sugar. Beat in egg and white. Sift in flour and fold together. Rest for 30 minutes.

Roll out and line a 10 inch tart case. Line with baking paper and fill with baking rice. Bake for 20 minutes at 180°C.

Allow to cool and remove rice and paper.

For the treacle tart filling

Mix all the ingredients together and fill the tart base. Bake at 150°C for 7 to 10 minutes.

For the toffee sauce

Melt butter and sugar. Bring to the boil then add cream. Bring to the boil once again and then cool and use. Serve with good quality clotted cream.

To serve

Assemble as in the picture.

Ingredients

Treacle Tart Base

100g caster sugar
125g unsalted butter
1 egg
1 egg white
250g plain flour

Treacle Tart Filling

1kg golden syrup
350g fresh breadcrumbs
1 lemon juice and zest

Toffee Sauce

100g unsalted butter
100g brown sugar
200ml double cream

240
TY MAWR MANSION COUNTRY HOUSE

Cilcennin, Lampeter, Ceredigion SA48 8DB

01570 470 033
www.tymawrmansion.co.uk

Located just 4 miles from the heritage Cardigan Bay coastline in the breathtaking surroundings of the Aeron Valley, Ty Mawr Mansion Country House and Restaurant is truly the best keep secret in Ceredigion.

Ty Mawr was a private house as recently as 2004, at which point it was refurbished to its former glory and today it offers warm and comfortable surroundings; a real home from home. All nine rooms and suites are individually decorated, with high-tech bathrooms and sumptuous furnishings to make this a truly special place to be.

With a focus on dining and relaxation, you will never find a wedding taking place during your stay. Why? Because our dedicated staff concentrate on you, the guest, to offer you the best experience possible.

With a background in fresh produce the restaurant at Ty Mawr Mansion was never going to be run-of-the-mill and with the help of Head Chef Gareth Morgan, Ty Mawr Mansion offers outstanding and imaginative food.

Gareth Morgan is not only a fully qualified lecturer but he is also an award-winning chef, having won 2 True Taste Awards. This local Welshman is extremely passionate about food and only uses local Welsh produce, with over 80% of ingredients coming from within a 10 mile radius.

With a modern, molecular slant to his cuisine his dishes are made to be savoured whilst taking in the relaxing ambiance and incredible views at Ty Mawr.

Another unique selling point at Ty Mawr Mansion is that we never resell a table, meaning your table is yours for the entire evening, allowing you to enjoy this talented chef's cuisine in an unhurried way. As well as this, after dinner you can while away the rest of your evening in our very own 27 seat private cinema.

With a background in fresh produce the restaurant at Ty Mawr Mansion was never going to be run-of-the-mill and with the help of Head Chef Gareth Morgan, Ty Mawr Mansion offers outstanding and imaginative food

HAM HOCK AND FORAGED WILD MUSHROOM VERRINE, DUCK EGG YOLK, WATERCRESS, BEETROOT VINEGAR FROTH VERRINE

SERVES 4

 Jim Barry 'The Lodge Hill' Riesling, Clare Valley 2010

Ingredients

2 ham hocks (on the bone)
2 bay leaves
4 sprigs fresh thyme
1tsp black peppercorns
1 onion (quartered)
200g wild mushrooms
50g gherkins (finely chopped)
20g flat leaf parsley (chopped)
20g chives (chopped)

4 duck eggs
Maldon sea salt

1 bunch watercress (keep a few leaves to garnish)

2 beetroots (cooked)
200ml white wine vinegar
2tsp soy lecithin

Method

For the ham hock

Place the ham hocks in a large pan along with the bay leaves, thyme, peppercorns and onion. Pour over enough cold water to cover then bring to the boil and simmer gently for 2-2½ hours, until the hocks are tender and flaky.

Clean the mushrooms and slice them before sautéing. Keep a few pieces separate to garnish.

Once the ham is cooked, leave the hocks in the liquid for about one hour to cool, then remove them and set aside. Strain the liquid into a clean pan (discard the solids) and boil vigorously for one hour to reduce the liquid by three-quarters to about 600ml. Remove the skin from the hocks then shred the meat and set it aside. Place the gherkins, chopped herbs and the mushrooms together and mix them well, adding seasoning as you do so. Pack them into a jam jar or terrine with the meat and press down firmly. Pour in the reduced liquid and allow to settle throughout the mixture. Leave to chill in the fridge for 2-4 hours.

For the duck egg yolk

Place the duck eggs in a waterbath for one hour at 64°C. Remove the egg yolk from the white and place into a ramekin to serve. Season with Maldon sea salt.

For the watercress dressing

Blanch the watercress and blitz to a purée in a food processor.

For the vinegar froth

Place the cooked beetroot in a food processor and purée. Keep some of the purée for garnish. Add vinegar to the rest and the soy lecithin. Blend and season.

To serve

Garnish and assemble as in the picture.

PAN FRIED CILCENNIN LAMB FILLET, BON-BON, SWEETCORN PURÉE, DAMSON FRITTERS AND JELLY, JUS

SERVES 4

 Viña Arana Reserva, La Rioja Alta, Rioja 2004

Ingredients

Lamb

micro herbs
4 x 200g reduced lamb jus
200g lamb fillet (vacuum packed)

Bon-Bon

240g lamb belly confit meat
4 eggs
50g flour
50g fine breadcrumbs

Sweetcorn Purée

250g sweetcorn (tinned or frozen)
milk

Damson Fritters - Tempura

3 tbsp plain flour
2 tbsp corn flour
1 tbsp baking powder
1 small bottle carbonated mineral water (ice cold)
3 damsons

Damson Jelly

200g fresh damsons purée
1g agar-agar

Method

For the lamb

Cook the lamb fillets at 56°C in a water bath then seal them in a hot pan and remove from the heat. Season and rest for 5 minutes then slice the lamb ready for presentation.

For the bon-bons

Mould the confit lamb into neat balls and then coat them in the plain flour, egg and breadcrumbs. Deep fry each coated bon-bon until golden brown then dry on paper and season ready for presentation.

For the sweetcorn purée

Place the sweetcorn in a blender and add milk. Blend to make a purée and season. Warm up and place into a small bottle ready to serve.

For damson fritters

Mix all the flour with a bit of the water to make a batter consistency. Remove the stones from the damsons then coat them in the batter and fry until crisp. Dry on a paper towel and season ready to serve.

For the damson jelly

Place the agar-agar in the damson purée and bring it to the boil. Blend well and place in a tray lined with clingfilm. When set, cut up into small squares ready for presentation.

To serve

Assemble as in the picture.

WARM CHOCOLATE MOUSSE, DOUGHNUTS, BUTTERMILK SORBET

SERVES 4

🍷 *Moscatel de Setúbal, Bacalhôa,*
Portugal 2005

Ingredients

Warm Mousse

200g dark chocolate
150g double cream
150g egg whites
isi container
2 isi cartridges

Doughnuts

7g sachet dried yeast
70g caster sugar
500g plain flour
315ml milk (tepid)
80g unsalted butter (softened)

Sugar Garnish

100g caster sugar
1 tsp ground cinnamon
½ tsp freshly grated nutmeg
½ tsp ground allspice

Buttermilk Sorbet

900ml fresh buttermilk
240g caster sugar
40g liquid glucose

Method

For the warm mousse

Melt the chocolate in the cream over a bain-marie. Separate the egg whites and add to the mixture. Pour the mixture into the isi container with 2 cartridges and keep warm.

For the doughnuts

Put the yeast in a bowl with a teaspoon of the caster sugar and mix in the warm milk. Stand in a warm place for about 15 minutes until the mixture becomes frothy.

In another bowl put the rest of the sugar, flour and butter. Add the yeast mixture and bring it all together, using your hands to mix it into ball. If it's too sticky, add a bit more flour. Knead the dough for 5 minutes until smooth and silky. Put it into a bowl, cover with a clean, damp cloth and leave to rise for about 1 hour.

Make your flavoured sugar by mixing the sugar and spices together in a bowl. When the dough has doubled in size give it a bit of punch, then, on a floured surface, roll the dough out until it's an even 1 cm/½ inch thickness. Using a little cutter (approximately 5 cm/2 inch diameter) cut out about 25 little circles and put them onto a greased baking tray to rise again. Make sure there is a sufficient gap between each of them. Cover with damp tea towel and leave them to rise for about 45 minutes.

When the dough has doubled in size again, make a little hole in the centre. Cook in a fryer at 160°C until golden brown. Then sprinkle them in the flavoured sugar.

For the buttermilk sorbet

Place the buttermilk in a saucepan and allow it to simmer gently until it has reduced by half (450ml).

When reduced, add sugar and glucose and stir until dissolved. Freeze in an ice-cream churner.

To serve

Assemble as in the picture.

250
TYDDYN LLAN

Llandrillo, nr. Corwen, Denbighshire, North Wales LL21 0ST

01490 440 264
www.tyddynllan.co.uk

With only a dozen bedrooms, Tyddyn Llan is a small, but elegant, Georgian country house set in the foothills of Snowdonia, run by husband and wife team Bryan and Susan Webb but it is also one of only four Michelin-starred restaurants in Wales. Born in Wales, Bryan's background was not in food. Bryan explains "I was brought up in a mining valley of Wales in a village called Crumlin. Although I had a very happy childhood, there was something inside me that wanted to move away and better myself. There was always the threat from my father that unless I did well at school I could get a job down the pit, which of course was the last thing I wanted. Too much like hard work! Little did I know then how hard you have to work to be a good chef" he jokes.

"My style is simple, honest food with bags of flavour; the kind of food you want to eat yourself. I would never serve something that I would not want to eat." The finest ingredients are of utmost importance in Bryan's cooking. "It has to be the very best even down to the basics, which is why no matter how much I love to buy locally if it's not good enough I look elsewhere. Our scallops are from Scotland as are our langoustine and wild smoked salmon. Lobsters and crabs travel from Cornwall, while fish arrives via Devon and the Label Anglais chicken comes from a farm in Essex. Even mozzarella is flown in once a week from Naples, via London, to our door. While all our meat is from local farms butchered at T.J Roberts in Bala, whom I have a fantastic relationship with, and all our needs are looked after well." Some of the cows and lambs even graze in the surrounding fields of Tyddyn Llan!

Bryan has found excellent ducks on a farm in south Wales and while local gardeners grow crops of beans and salads, farms on the Wirral supply beautiful watercress, rocket and micro herbs, asparagus and soft fruit.

Nine years, a book and a Michelin-star later, together with wife Susan who runs the front of house, they have achieved a huge amount of respect and accolades at Tyddyn Llan. "But it doesn't get any easier! To succeed you need lots of passion and a love for this business, to be able to give all the effort that it takes to run a successful restaurant, as without it you are just another restaurant. So no plans for the future, just keep on doing what we do as somewhere along the way we must be getting it right."

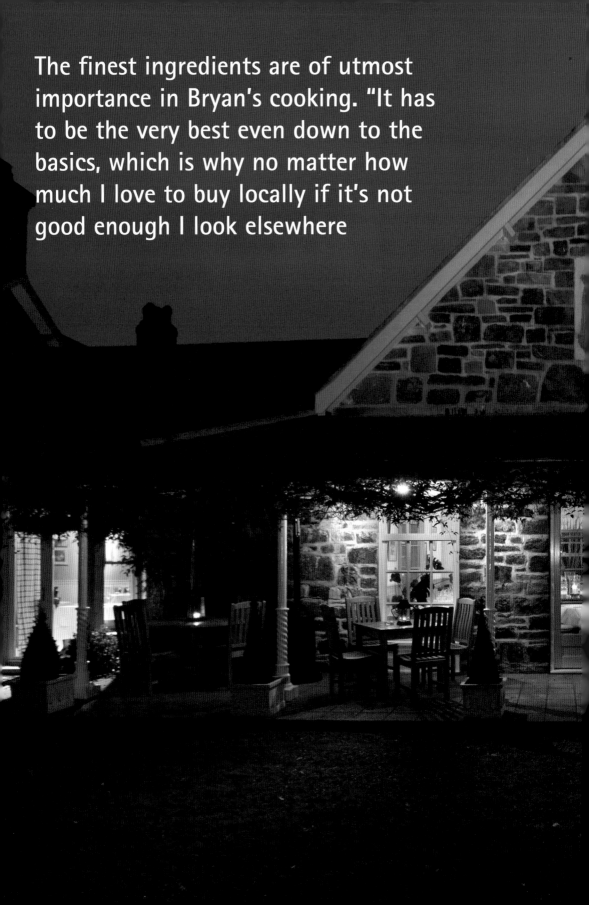

The finest ingredients are of utmost importance in Bryan's cooking. "It has to be the very best even down to the basics, which is why no matter how much I love to buy locally if it's not good enough I look elsewhere

GRILLED RED MULLET WITH CHILLI AND GARLIC OIL

SERVES 4

🍷 *Rully 2007 Jean-Claude Boisset, Nuits-St-Georges, Burgundy, France*

Ingredients

Aubergine Purée

500g cooked aubergine flesh (about 3 aubergines)
2 to 3 cloves of garlic
juice of ½ a large lemon
½ tsp of ground cumin
1 tbsp of tahini
100ml extra virgin olive oil
salt and pepper

Grilled Red Mullet

4 large Red Mullet (about 500g each, filleted)
olive oil
sea salt (Halen Môn is very good)

Chilli and Garlic Oil

3 cloves garlic (chopped)
2 anchovy fillets
½ tbsp chilli flakes
2 tbsp sunflower oil
75ml extra virgin olive oil
parsley (chopped)

Method

For the aubergine purée

First, grill the aubergines on a solid top or baked in the oven until soft. When cool, peel them and leave to drain in a colander over a bowl, with a weighted plate on top for 1 hour. After this time place all the ingredients in a food processor and puree them. Slowly add the olive oil and check the seasoning.

For the grilled red mullet

Heat the grill to the maximum. Season the fillets of fish with salt and pepper and place on a tray lightly oiled with olive oil. Place the fish onto the tray with the skin facing up.

Put the fillet under the grill and heat until just cooked. Warm the aubergine purée and place a spoonful into four heated bowls. Mix a little chopped parsley into the dressing and pour a small amount around the purée.

Place the cooked fish on top of the purée and serve.

For the chilli and garlic oil

Heat the garlic, anchovy and chilli flakes in the sunflower oil until the anchovy melts. Remove from the heat.

Add the olive oil and leave to cool.

To serve

Assemble as in the picture.

ROAST PIGEON WITH BRAISED BUTTER BEANS AND WILD MUSHROOMS

SERVES 4

Rioja Crianza 2007 Dinastia Vivanco, Briones, La Rioja, Spain

Ingredients

4 large squab pigeon
2 shallots (finely chopped)
4 bay leaves
4 sprigs of thyme
salt and pepper
40g butter

300g butter beans (soaked overnight and simmer in water with a bay leaf, a stick of celery, but no salt for about two hours until soft)

150g wild mushrooms (cleaned)
2 shallots (roughly chopped)
50ml brandy
100ml madeira
100ml white wine
2 bay leaves, sprig of thyme, parsley stalks
150ml chicken stock
150ml veal or beef stock

Method

If the pigeons have not been gutted, remove them and keep the livers. Cut the feet, but not all the way though, twist and pull and the feet will come off together with the sinew from the drum stick. Remove the wishbone and the neck bones and keep to one side.

Divide the shallots between the four pigeon cavities, together with the thyme and bay leaves. Season with salt and pepper and push a cocktail stick though the legs to secure them.

Fry any scrapes of bones with the roughly chopped shallots for a few minutes, then add the brandy and bring to the boil, then add the Madeira and white wine. Reduce by half, add the stocks and simmer for 30 minutes, strain and reduce to a slightly thick sauce.

Pre-heat the oven to 220°C. Place the pigeons in a tray, season with salt and pepper and spread the butter over the breasts of the pigeons. Roast in a hot oven for 8 minutes, baste with any juices and butter and turn them over so that they are breast down and cook for a further 4 minutes for a pink bird and 6 to 8 minutes for well done.

Remove from the oven and place on a warm tray to rest. Pour away any fat, deglaze with the sauce scraping up the goodness left in the tray and strain back into a clean saucepan.

To serve

Reheat the butter beans and season with salt and pepper, cook the wild mushrooms in some hot olive oil and season. Remove the legs and cook in the oven for 4 minutes. While you carve the breasts, arrange the beans and mushrooms on four heated plates. Arrange the breasts on top and finally the legs. Pour the sauce over and when in season garnish with some skinned broad beans.

ALMOND TART WITH PRUNE AND MASCARPONE ICE CREAM

SERVES 4

🍷 *Moscato d'Asti di Strevi 2010 Contero, Strevi, Piedmont, Italy*

Ingredients

Almond Tart Pastry

250g flour
160g butter
1 whole egg
a pinch of salt and sugar
1tbsp milk

Almond Tart Filling

100g softened butter
100g caster sugar
2 large free range eggs
50g ground almonds
50g whole, blanched almonds (ground in a food processor)
20g flaked almonds
150g stoned dried prunes
1 egg (lightly beaten)

Prune and Mascarpone Ice Cream

250ml cream
250ml milk
1 split vanilla pod
280g sugar
6 egg yolks
250g mascarpone
10ml Armagnac
10 stoned prunes (chopped)

Method

For the pastry

First, make the pastry in a food processor or by hand. Blend together the flour, butter, salt and sugar until it resembles breadcrumbs. Now tip them into a large bowl and add the egg and milk, gently mixing until it is well amalgamated. Wrap in clingfilm and chill for 1 hour before rolling out.

Pre heat the oven to 170°C.

Roll out the pastry as thinly as possible and line a loose-bottomed, 20cm x 4cm tart tin. Line the pastry with a large sheet of clingfilm or tin foil and fill with baking beans or any dried pluses such as haricot beans. Leave to rest for 20 minutes and then bake for 20 minutes. Remove from the oven and take out the foil or film with the beans to keep for future use (if you wish to do so). Brush the base with beaten egg to form a seal and bake for a further 5 minutes.

For the filling

Turn the oven temperature down to 150°C.

Beat the butter and sugar together in an electric mixer until light and fluffy. Add one egg and continue beating, then add the other egg and beat again until entirely incorporated. Add the two types of ground almonds and carefully fold them in.

Place the prunes onto the base of the pastry case and fill with the almond mix, sprinkle with the flaked almonds and bake for 1 hour and 10 minutes. Switch off the oven and leave to cool with the door ajar for 15 minutes; it is best serve warm with some thick cream.

For the prune and mascarpone ice cream

Warm the milk, cream and vanilla.

Boil the sugar with a little water to 106°C and pour over the egg yolks and add the hot milk and cream.

When cool, strain through a sieve and mix with 250g mascarpone cheese.

Add the prunes and Armagnac.

Churn in the ice cream machine.

To serve

Assemble as in the picture.

260
THE WALNUT TREE

Llanddewi Skirrid, Abergavenny, Monmouthshire NP7 8AW

01873 852 797
www.thewalnuttreeinn.com

The Walnut Tree has been a beacon of good food in South Wales for nearly fifty years. It's first incarnation was as an idiosynchratic and exciting Italian restaurant owned and run by Franco and Ann Taruschio. A brief and successful stint from Stephen Terry, now of the Hardwick, followed their retirement but then all went awry and a grim visit from Gordon Ramsay's kitchen nightmares telly programme provided the coup de grace so the place closed.

Shaun Hill took over the Walnut Tree in 2007, cooking alongside Roger Brook, and whilst the kitchen now reflects a different style the restaurant still holds the informal and easygoing atmosphere of its past. It offers proper dining and drinking in an informal setting; for a glass of good wine with a plate of something, through to a full lunch or dinner!

The menu is an eclectic mix, based on personal taste and sound cooking techniques using excellent core ingredients: local where feasible and carefully chosen. The success of this large operation is down to a brigade of chefs. It is not just Shaun cooking solo at the stove. Some of these chefs worked with Shaun before and some worked at The Walnut Tree in its former glory days.

Most independent guides have awarded some gong or other to the place and it seems that the restaurant is once more a fixture amongst Wales' eating out fraternity.

Shaun Hill took over the Walnut Tree in 2007, cooking alongside Roger Brook, and whilst the kitchen now reflects a different style the restaurant still holds the informal and easygoing atmosphere of its past

BRAISED TURBOT WITH COB NUT CRUST AND CLAM BROTH

SERVES 4

🍷 *Vintage Tunina 2006 Silvio Jermann from Friuli in North East Italy*

Ingredients

4 x 150g turbot fillet

Stuffing/Topping

75g fresh breadcrumbs
2 shallots (chopped)
40g unsalted butter
10 cob nuts (peeled and chopped)
2 tbsp (chopped parsley)

Clam Broth

30 clams in their shells
50ml white wine
1 tbsp crème fraîche
50g unsalted butter
1 tsp lemon juice and a few dashes tabasco
12 small potatoes (boiled and sliced in two)

Method

We use turbot fillets, which are of course gorgeous for this dish but then we are a reasonably expensive restaurant. The same method will work fine for cod, halibut or hake fillet if you prefer. Plaice or lemon sole fillets are too fragile. In fact the freshness and condition of any white fish is the most important factor. This is an early autumn dish when cob nuts are in season and both cockles and clams plentiful. Chopped button mushrooms will work instead but not be quite as good of course.

For the stuffing

Make the stuffing by sweating the chopped shallots for a minute in the butter then by adding the nuts breadcrumbs and parsley. You should have a firm but soft stuffing. Season with salt and pepper.

For the clam broth

Make the clam broth by heating the clams in white wine in a lidded saucepan until they open. Stir in the crème fraîche and then stir in the butter to thicken. Taste the broth which should have the consistency of thin soup then add the potatoes some lemon juice and Tabasco to enliven it.

To serve

Sear the fish in a hot pan then press on the stuffing,

Bake for 5 minutes so that the fish is just cooked then pour over the clam broth.

HARE IN PUFF PASTRY WITH MOREL MUSHROOMS AND GAME GRAVY

SERVES 4

Nuits St Georges 2002 Domaine de l'Arlot from Burgundy

Ingredients

2 hares
25g dried morel mushrooms
1 tbsp plain flour
1 onion (peeled and chopped)
1 leek (washed then chopped)
2 fat cloves of garlic (peeled then crushed)
1 tbsp tomato passata
¼ bottle decent red wine

1 sheet puff pastry cut into 4 rectangles

Method

Hare is regularly served jugged, a strange word that signifies braised then thickened with its own blood. All quite nasty and often leaving a taste in the mouth like a visit to the dentist. Meat from the hare's saddle, however, is delicate and full flavoured, excellent served quite rare. The leg meat is really best slow-cooked or braised. The foreleg and shoulder is best discarded or used in stock since it is quite tough with little meat to reward the hours of cooking needed to render it palatable.

The bonus is that the braised leg will yield great gravy so the dish is reasonably self contained needing neither veal stocks nor any other restaurant staple. The puff pastry case lends a delicate texture as well as providing a handy home for the braised leg. Ready made puff pastry has improved beyond recognition over the past ten years so buy it rather than make it.

For the hares

Cut the legs from the hares then bone them. This needn't be done in a surgical manner for you are going to cut the meat into smallish dice afterwards.

Dice the meat then dust with flour. Use a heavy casserole pan to sear the meat in hot oil alongside the chopped vegetables and garlic. Add tomato passata then red wine and top up with a little water and the morel mushrooms. Add a little water if the meat is not covered. Place a lid on the pan and then braise slowly until the meat is completely tender, about an hour and a half.

Bake the puff pastry rectangles in a hot oven 200°C.

Cut away the fillets from the saddle and brush with olive oil. Sear in a hot pan then transfer to a roasting tray and roast briefly for about 5 minutes until rare.

To serve

Spoon the braised meat and morel mushrooms into the pastry cases. Carve the fillets from the saddle into long strips and lay across the top. Spoon all cooking juices on top then serve.

We usually serve mashed celeriac or roasted salsify alongside some Savoy cabbage with this dish. The pastry will provide all the starch needed.

ORANGE AND ALMOND CAKE

SERVES 6-8

Capitelli 2006 Roberto Anselmi – from Veneto in Italy

Ingredients

2 medium sized oranges
250g caster sugar
6 eggs
250g ground almonds
1 tbsp baking powder

Syrup

50g granulated sugar (boiled together with
50ml water then cooled)
2 tbsp Grand Marnier or Cointreau

Method

This cake will serve as a pudding not just an accompaniment to a pot of tea. It is softened after baking with syrup and grand Marnier in much the same way as a rum baba but contains no flour so handy for those on a gluten free diet.

Boil the oranges in water for about three hours, until they are very soft.

Cool then halve and scrape away the pips.

Blend in a food processer then drain away as much liquid as you can. You will need around 250g to 300g of chopped pulp and skin in total. It is important that this has been squeezed as dry as possible.

Whisk the eggs, sugar, baking powder and almonds together for a minute if you are using an electric whisk or for three minutes if whisking by hand. Add the orange then whisk again for the same amount of time.

Line an 8 x 2 ½ inch tin with baking parchment then pour in the batter.

Bake on the middle shelf of an oven preheated to 150°C for one hour.

Allow to cool before spiking the top surface of the cake all over with a skewer. Soak with the syrup mixed together with the Grand Marnier.

To serve

Serve with either a scoop of crème fraîche or a scoop of crème fraîche ice cream.

Bob's your uncle!

Y POLYN

Capel Dewi, Carmarthenshire SA32 7LH

01267 290 000
www.ypolynrestaurant.co.uk

Carmarthenshire, the garden of Wales, is a county of green, sheep-dotted, hills and fertile valleys. Tucked away in the Towy valley between the county town of Carmarthen and chic Llandeilo sits Y Polyn. A country pub turned restaurant, now owned by husband and wife team Mark and Susan Manson, Y Polyn is a welcoming informal place to enjoy the fruits of Wales's farming bounty. They aren't trying to be cutting-edge or post-modern. You won't find foams, gels and technical wizardry on the plate. What you will find is beautiful produce, cooked simply and with respect. Salt marsh lamb, Welsh beef and free range, rare breed pork are highlights of the well balanced menu.

They are very keen to avoid pretention at Y Polyn. Tables are mismatching bare wood, tablecloths are banished, our staff wear tee shirts and jeans and you can pour your own wine. Perhaps the words shabby-chic best describe the décor here. The bar area offers an opportunity to sample Otley's fine cask ales or ask Scottish owner Mark to recommend one of his fine collection of malt whiskies.

As chef and owner Susan says "We're not interested in reinventing the wheel here. We like the simple things in life, but we like them done as well as they can be".

Warmth and a lack of pretention characterise service at Y Polyn. Staff enjoy working here and the friendly team want their guests to feel at ease and well looked after. Informality in both food and welcome are key to the Y Polyn experience

ABERDARON CRAB CAKES, PICKLED VEGETABLE RELISH

SERVES 6

🍷 *Berton Estates, The White Viognier 2010 Eden Valley, South Australia*

Ingredients

2 spring onions (white only) (washed and finely sliced)
1 red chilli (deseeded and finely chopped)
1.5 cm piece ginger root (peeled and finely chopped)
juice of half an orange
juice of half a lemon
salt and pepper to taste
300g picked white crab meat
200g brown crab meat
25g panko breadcrumbs
1 egg

To Coat

panko breadcrumbs
plain flour
2 eggs

Pickled Vegetable Relish

1 red onion
1 red pepper (seeds and stalk removed)
1 yellow pepper (seeds and stalk removed)
½ red chilli (seeds removed)
1 stick celery
1 carrot (peeled and chopped)
10 salted anchovies

Dressing for Relish

1 tsp Dijon mustard
1 tbsp clear honey
juice of half an orange
100ml red wine vinegar
200ml extra virgin olive oil
salt and pepper to taste
1 tbsp parsley (finely chopped)

Method

For the relish

Make the relish first so the flavours have time to develop and the vegetables soften a little in the dressing.

Wash, peel and finely dice all the vegetables and add the finely chopped anchovies.

Whisk together all the ingredients for the dressing keeping the parsley until you are ready to serve the dish as it will discolour. Add the vegetables and leave in a cool place for an hour or two.

For the crab cakes

Fold together all the ingredients for the crab cakes and divide into 18 small balls. Flour, egg and crumb the cakes using the coating ingredients. Once coated, gently flatten the balls into crab cake shapes.

To cook the cakes, heat a frying pan with a little oil and butter until the butter just starts to foam. Cook each side until golden brown and finish in a hot oven for approximately 7 minutes until hot all the way through.

To serve

Add the parsley to the relish. Spoon a portion of relish on to each of six plates and add three cakes per portion. You can add some dressed salad leaves as a garnish if you like.

MARGAM PARK VENISON LOIN WITH VENISON RAGU AND PARSNIP PURÉE

SERVES 6

🍷 *Châteauneuf Du Pape, Les Cailloux, 2006 Brunel*

Ingredients

Venison Loin

6 x 130-150g pieces venison loin
½ bottle red wine
1 carrot (peeled), 1 celery stick, 1 white onion
6 cloves garlic
2 bay leaves

Venison Ragu

450g haunch of venison (diced 1cm cubes)
2 small white onions, 2 carrots (peeled)
1 leek (white only)
6 cloves garlic
2 sticks celery, 2 bay leaves
1 tbsp tomato puree
¼ bottle red wine
500ml chicken stock
oil for frying
salt and pepper to taste

Venison Sauce

50g 1cm venison haunch (diced)
1 small carrot (peeled)
1 small white onion, 1 stick celery
1 small leek (white only)
4 cloves garlic
1 bay leaf
2 sprigs thyme
1 tsp tomato purée
¼ bottle red wine
1 litre chicken stock
oil for frying

Parsnip Purée

900g parsnips
125g salted butter
(to make purée, boil in salt water until soft then purée)

Parsnip Crisps

1 large parsnip

Method

For the venison

Roughly chop the vegetables and marinade the pieces of loin overnight, in a fridge, in a plastic container with the wine, vegetables and herbs.

For the venison ragu

Finely dice one carrot, celery stick, one onion and the leek. Blitz the remaining carrot, celery, onion and garlic to a fine purée in a food processor. Preheat your oven to 150°C.

Brown the diced venison in small batches and set aside. Add the finely diced vegetables and sweat them until they have softened, then add the tomato purée and cook for a minute or two. Add the browned venison. Reduce. Add the red wine and cook for 5 minutes. Add the chicken stock and bay leaves and bring to the boil. Put the lid on and transfer to your oven for approximately 4 hours. Check every ½ hour and add some more stock if the mix is getting too dry. Remove then allow to cool. Refrigerate until needed.

For the venison sauce

Brown the venison well. Add the vegetables and cook until lightly browned. Add the tomato purée and add the red wine. Reduce. Add the chicken stock and herbs. Bring to boiling point then simmer and cook the sauce until it has reduced by two thirds. Strain the sauce through a fine sieve and refrigerate until needed.

For the parsnip crisps

Peel and trim the ends of the parsnip. Carefully peel long strips from top to bottom with a potato peeler. Lay one sheet of paper on one tray then lay the parsnip strips on the paper and sparingly brush each strip with oil. Season. Lay the 2nd paper-lined baking sheet on top. Put the whole sandwich into a preheated oven at 180°C for about 5 minutes until the strips are golden brown. Keep checking, the parsnip strips burn very quickly! Reserve the cooked crisps until needed.

To serve

Remove the venison loin pieces from the marinade and, pat them dry and season. Heat and, when the butter foams, add the venison pieces and brown on all sides. Put the pan into a preheated oven at 180°C for about 3-4 minutes. Turn each piece over and cook for a further 3-4 minutes. Remove and rest in foil for 5 minutes. Whilst the venison loins are cooking, heat up the ragu, parsnip purée and the venison sauce in separate pans and check for seasoning. On each of six plates spoon 1 tablespoon of purée and a helping of the ragu. Slice the loins into 3-4 slices then arrange on the plate. Garnish with a few parsnip crisps.

TOFFEE APPLE CRUMBLE KNICKERBOCKER GLORY

SERVES 6

🍷 *Noble One Botrytis Semillon 2006, De Bortoli*

Ingredients

Toffee Sauce

300g caster sugar
800ml double cream
200g salted butter

Toffee Ice Cream

1.1 litres double cream
8 egg whites
220g caster sugar
half of the previously made cold toffee sauce

Crumble Mix

100g salted butter
75g Demerara sugar
175g plain flour

Tuile Wafers

150g flaked almonds
150g caster sugar
60g plain flour
40g melted butter
2 egg whites, 1 egg yolk

Apple Compote

2-3 large Bramley apples
100g caster sugar
1 tsp ground ginger
1 tsp ground cinnamon

Method

For the toffee sauce

Finely dice the butter and reserve in a fridge. Warm the cream gently in a saucepan.

In a heavy-based saucepan, dissolve the sugar over a low heat then increase the heat until the sugar has turned into a deep golden caramel. Be very careful not to burn your caramel. Carefully add the warm cream a little at a time (it will spit and seethe). Once all the cream is added, whisk in the diced butter. Remove from the heat, pour into a metal container and allow to cool.

For the toffee ice cream

Whisk the egg whites until stiff. Keep whisking and add the sugar to make a meringue, then add the toffee sauce. Separately whisk the double cream to the soft peaks stage. Gently fold the cream into the toffee meringue mixture. Freeze the mixture for 24 hours.

For the crumble mix

Preheat your oven to 180°C. Using your fingertips, rub together the flour and butter until sandy in texture. Stir in the sugar. Tip onto a baking sheet and then bake. Every 5 minutes break up with a spoon. Keep cooking and turning until the mix is golden brown. You are aiming for the texture of coarse sand.

For the tuile wafers

You can make the mixture the day before (store it in the fridge) but the tuiles are best made on the day you want to eat them as they do go soggy quickly. Mix all the dry ingredients together, add the egg yolk, then the 2 egg whites and finally mix in the melted butter. Line a large baking sheet with baking parchment and spoon teaspoon sized balls on the paper. Flatten these balls out with wet fingers (so they don't stick) into 1mm thick large ovals. Leave a gap of about 1cm between each tuile to allow for spreading. Bake for 5-10 minutes until the tuiles are golden brown. Remove from the oven and cut each oval into halves lengthways while still hot. Cool on a rack until needed.

For the apple compote

Peel and core the apples and chop into 1-2cm dice. Cook over a low heat in a heavy-based saucepan until the apples are soft and the sugar has dissolved.

To assemble

Ideally these should be served in old fashioned long Knickerbocker Glory glasses but Sundae glasses would do in a pinch. Layer the ingredients up in the glass; apple, crumble mix, toffee sauce and ice cream until you reach the top. You should manage about three layers of each. Top off with a bit of toffee sauce and garnish with two tuile halves.

280
YE OLDE BULLS HEAD INN

Castle Street, Beaumaris, Anglesey LL58 8AP

01248 810 329
www.bullsheadinn.co.uk

Ye Olde Bulls Head, Beaumaris, established in 1472 and re-built in 1617, is an historic coaching inn on the coast of the Isle of Anglesey. It has all the character you would expect, to reflect its great age, including the biggest simple hinged gate in the UK. Past guests, Cromwell, and Charles Dickens would surely appreciate the 25 years the present owners have spent ensuring that the expectations required by the modern traveller are not just met, but exceeded in every way.

In addition to the comfort of the luxurious bedrooms is the traditional public bar which is liberally decorated with antiques and serves hand pulled real ale. There is also a busy bustling modern brasserie and 'The Loft' restaurant.

Hefin Roberts and his team have gained entries for 'The Loft' in all the major food guides, and he weaves modern British magic in the kitchen. He has lived and worked in North Wales all his life, and is knowledgeable and passionate about using all the ingredients available locally. Anglesey is rightly known as 'Mon Mam Cymru', 'The Mother of Wales' because of the fertility of the island. It provides a range of wonderfully diverse and exceptionally high quality produce.

An evening in 'The Loft' will begin in the elegant lounge where canapés and drinks are served. You can then peruse the menu and choose from a list of 180 wines which includes both the classic and more esoteric offerings. Your carefully prepared five course dinner in 'The Loft' showcases the finest local produce ranging from Menai mussels, lobster, scallops, or sea bass from coastal waters to Welsh beef, lamb and game from the Island's pastures. Whilst Hefin's approach is unashamedly contemporary, this is underpinned by his desire to treat such fine quality ingredients with the respect they deserve. 400 years ago a coaching inn is where you would relax, eat, drink, and be well looked after. That's exactly the service that the Bulls Head still provides today.

An evening in 'The Loft' will begin in the elegant lounge where canapés and drinks are served. You can then peruse the menu and choose from a list of 180 wines which includes both the classic and more esoteric offerings

SEARED KING SCALLOP, CURRIED MUSSELS, CRISP CRAB, CRAYFISH TAILS AND LEMON HOLLANDAISE

SERVES 4

Saint Joseph Blanc, André Perret
Rhône Valley, France

Ingredients

8 large king scallops
8 fresh crayfish
500g fresh mussels

Lemon Hollandaise

2 eggs
250g butter
white wine vinegar
2 lemons (zest of 1 whole lemon and juice of half a lemon)

Crab Fritter

1 fresh crab
50g butter
50g plain flour
250ml milk
1 lemon
sprinkle of coriander (chopped)

Fennel Purée

1 fennel
1 clove garlic
20g butter
salt and pepper
10g fennel seeds

Curried Sauce

garlic
fennel seeds
1 shallot
spices - cumin, turmeric, ginger, chilli, coriander, coriander seeds, saffron, garam masala, double cream
knob of butter

Method

For the fennel purée

Peel the fennel, then remove the outer leaves and peel again. Continue this process until you reach the heart of the fennel. Once all the fennel leaves are peeled, very finely dice the fennel and set aside. Purée one clove of garlic. Poach and soften the fennel and garlic in the butter. Season with salt, pepper and fennel seeds. This should not take any longer than 8 minutes. Once softened, blend and pass through a sieve.

For the curried sauce

Toast the spices to increase the flavours then add a knob of butter, one finely diced shallot and the garlic purée. Sauté until the shallots are soft then add the double cream.

Reduce, test the seasoning then refrigerate.

For the lemon hollandaise

In a large metal bowl separate the egg, discard the whites and put the yolks in a bowl with a touch of water. Clarify the butter until the oil separates. Reduce the white wine vinegar and add the reduction to the yolks. Start whisking until light and fluffy and until it has doubled in size then keep whisking and gently pour the clarified butter onto the yolks until all the butter has been incorporated. Ensure the white sediment left over stays in the pan. Add the lemon zest and lemon juice into the hollandaise. Reserve until later.

For the crab fritter

Begin by making a bechamel sauce. Melt the butter and add to the flour, beat in until combined into a roux. Warm the milk and stir into the roux, bit by bit (a third at a time). Stir continuously so that the mixture doesn't go lumpy. Cook for 20 minutes and allow to cool. Meanwhile cook the crab for 5 minutes in rapidly boiling salted water. Then take out and leave to cool. Once cooled crack the claws and open the shell. Take the brown and white meat, discard the shells and fold both the crab meats into the bechamel. Season, and add a good squeeze of lemon juice then add the coriander. Cover with clingfilm and refrigerate until set. Once cooled, shape into balls (roughly 10-15g). Then panne (flour, eggs, breadcrumbs).

To serve

Sear the scallops by frying in a hot pan with a dash of oil. Cook for around a minute on each side, until golden brown. While the scallops are cooking, gently warm the mussels in the curried sauce. Then sauté the crayfish, adding a squeeze of lemon and a knob of butter to caramelise. Finally deep fry the crab fritters. Assemble as in the picture.

FILLET OF WELSH BEEF 'MEAT & POTATO PIE', WATERCRESS PURÉE, CREAMED CABBAGE, GLAZED VEGETABLES, PEPPERCORN JUS

SERVES 4

🍷 *Malbec, J.Alberto*
Rio Negro Valley, Patagonia

Ingredients

4 x 170g fillets of beef
1 oxtail
4 baking potatoes
4 carrots
8 asparagus
16 fine beans
1 swede
300g spinach
300g watercress
300ml beef jus
green peppercorns
20g tarragon
2 shallots

Method

Brown and braise your oxtail well in advance, this will take approximately 2 hours. Flake the meat off the bone when thoroughly cooked. Season the oxtail and reduce until the mixture is nice and sticky. Set aside.

Cut and shape the potato and braise in the stock. Place the oxtail mixture onto the potato, cut the pastry with a lattice cutter and lay the pastry over the oxtail and potato. Glaze with the egg and season.

Trim your fillet of beef and tie up into the sizes you like. Leave in the fridge until required.

Sauté the spinach with the watercress and add some fresh, grated nutmeg. Season with salt and pepper and add a knob of butter. Place in a blender and blend until perfectly smooth. Recheck seasoning.

Cut and pre cook the specified vegetables then refresh them in iced water.

Add diced sauté shallots and green peppercorns to your jus. Reduce jus until it achieves the right taste and consistency. Pan-fry the fillet for 4 minutes each side and leave to rest.

To serve

Saute the vegetables, season and add fresh chopped tarragon. Warm the purée and roast the potato and oxtail for 5 minutes at 170°C. Serve immediately.

TREACLE TART

SERVES 4

Noble Harvest, Lilly Pilly
Riverina, Australia

Ingredients

Treacle Tart

200g beurre noissette (browned butter)
180g egg yolk
100g double cream
10g salt
500g golden syrup (warmed)
150g white breadcrumbs
zest of one whole lemon
75ml lemon juice

Chopped Walnuts

walnuts (a handful)
250g milk

Chantilly Cream

250g double cream
1 vanilla pod
25g icing sugar

1 banana

Method

For the tart

Mix the butter with the warmed golden syrup. Mix in the yolks, cream and salt. Add the breadcrumbs, lemon juice and zest. Set into moulds and cook at 180°C for 20 minutes.

For the chopped walnuts

Poach the walnuts in the milk for 2 minutes and then remove from the heat. Leave this to cool. Wearing gloves and using a paring knife, peel the skin from the walnuts and keep the milk that was used to poach the walnuts to use as sauce later.

Once the walnuts are peeled dice them up gently and reserve for later use.

For the caramelised banana

Sprinkle caster sugar onto the sliced banana and caramelise using a blow torch or by placing under a grill.

For the chantilly cream

Whip the double cream and add the icing sugar and vanilla pod then refrigerate.

To serve

Heat the leftover milk, add a sprinkle of caster sugar and gently warm but don't go over 70°C. Then blend with a hand blender creating as much froth as possible. Sit the tart in the middle of a bowl, add the chopped walnuts on top, followed by the caramelised banana. Quenelle and add the chantilly cream. Spoon the milk froth around the tart and finish with a banana crisp as pictured.

290
RELISH WALES LARDER

BAKERY

BACHELDRE WATERMILL
N Bacheldre Watermill, Churchstoke, Montgomery,
Powys, SY15 6TE.
01588 620489
www.bacheldremill.co.uk

*Bacheldre Watermill produces both traditional and more
modern varieties of mill-ground flour using equipment
which is hundreds of years old.*

CAROLINE'S REAL BREAD COMPANY
The Old Vicarage Bakery, Merthyr
Cynog, Brecon, Powys LD3 9SD
01874 690378
www.carolinesrealbreadcompany.co.uk

*Caroline's Real Bread Company makes the widest variety of
bread, drawing inspiration from all around the world.*

POPTY CARA
Home Farm House, Lawrenny,
Kilgetty, Pembrokeshire SA68 0PN
01646 651690
www.poptycara.co.uk

*Daniel and Melanie Ives established Popty Cara in 1993.
They sell traditional cakes and puddings which are made
fresh to order. Daniel and Melanie Ives established Popty
Cara in 1993.*

BEVERAGES

BOUTINOT
Brook House, Northenden Road, Gatley, Cheshire SK8
4DN
0161 9081300
www.boutinot.com

*Boutinot is a major international wine business based
in the UK. With a portfolio of over 800 wines, they are
exclusive agents for around 150 producers around the
world and notably, have their own wine production sites in
both the northern and southern hemispheres.*

BEVERAGES

GWYNT CIDER
Llest Farm, Pontypridd, RCT, CF38 2PW
01443 209852
www.gwyntcider.com

Producers of ciders such as the award-winning 'Black Dragon',

LYSH
Berthfawr, Dolanog, Welshpool, Powys, SY21 0LW
07866 547894
www.lysh.co.uk

Producers of Damson Gin and Sloe & Almond Gin Liqueurs.

OTLEY BREWING COMPANY
Unit 42, Albion Industrial Estate, Cilfynydd, Pontypridd, CF37 4NX
01443 480555
www.otleybrewing.co.uk

The Brewery originated back in 2005 when the idea was to produce award winning-beers the likes of which had not been done in Wales before.

PEMBROKESHIRE TEA COMPANY
44a Stepney Street, Llanelli, SA15 3TR
01437 708090
www.pembrokeshiretea.co.uk

Hand blended in Pembrokeshire using imported and locally grown ingredients, The Pembrokeshire Tea range offers a selection of high quality teas.

PENARTH ESTATE WELSH WINES
Penarth Vineyard, Pool Road, Newton, Montgomeryshire, Powys, SY16 3AN
01686 610383
www.welshwine.co.uk

Penarth Estate sparkling wines have been produced in the traditional way; two years in stainless-steel tanks on lees and a 12 month bottle maturation create a wine that will compare favourably to its French counterparts.

PENDERYN DISTILLERY
The Welsh Whisky Company, Penderyn, CF44 9JW
www.welsh-whisky.co.uk

The Penderyn Distilery produces high quality Welsh wysgi that can be found on sale throughout the UK.

TOMOS WATKIN'S BREWERY
Unit 3, Century Park, Swansea Enterprise Park, Swansea, SA6 8RP
www.tomoswatkin.com

Tomos Watkin Brewery offers a wide selection of Welsh ales and ciders.

RODNEY DENSEM WINES LTD
4 Pillory Street, Nantwich, Cheshire, CW5 5BD
01270 626999
www.rodneydensemwines.com

Rodney Densem Wines was established in 1972 by Rodney and Margie Densem as an Independent Wine Business. They concentrated on marketing an individual and exciting collection of personally selected wines .

Ysgyryd Fawr, Abergavenny

CONFECTIONERY

CASTLE CHOCOLATES (WALES) LTD
Unit 9, Venture Wales, Bedwas House Industrial Estate,
Caerphilly CF83 8GF
02920 882229
www.castlechocolates.co.uk

This is a company that was created by chocolate lovers for chocolate lovers.

THE CHOCOLATE HOUSE
Unit 35, Business Development Centre, Main
Avenue, Trefforest Industrial Estate, Pontypridd,
CF37 5UR
01443 844221
www.chocolate-house.co.uk

The home of delicious, award winning chocolates. All the chocolates are handmade using the finest ingredients, natural flavours and preservatives.

CLAM'S CAKES
Lewis Parry House, Unit 4a, Elvicta Business Park,
Crickhowell, Powys, NP8 1DF
01873 812283
www.clamscakes.co.uk

Great Taste and True Taste Award winning cakes, including traditional Bara Birth, delivered to your home. We are a small dedicated team of 20 people making handmade cakes for discerning customers. We have stayed true to our origins; cracking real eggs, using real ingredients, baked by individual people, and all of our cakes are hand decorated.

COCO BEAN
Gower Heritage Centre, Parkmill, Gower Peninsular,
SA3 2EH
07919 077187
www.cocobeanwales.com

Truffles, brownies and cupcakes available at the Gower Heritage Centre and online. their award winning Pâté, potted beef, frozen ready meals.

GOWER COTTAGE BROWNIES
Gower Cottage, Higher Green, Reynoldston, Gower
SA3 1AD
01792 390011
www.gowercottagebrownies.co.uk

Gower Cottage's esteemed brownies come carefully presented and make a great gift for any occasion.

KID ME NOT
Ffynnongrech Farm, Talley, Llandeilo, Carmarthenshire,
SA19 7BZ
01558 685935
www.kidmenot.co.uk

Everything from yoghurt and cheese to fudge and chocolate made with delicious goat's milk, with no artificial colouring or flavouring.

PEMBERTON'S CHOCOLATE FARM
Llanboidy, Carmarthenshire, SA34 0EX
01994 448800
www.welshchocolatefarm.com

Find out how chocolate is made the traditional way.

EDIBLE FLOWERS

LEAF PRODUCE LTD
Blaenarfon, Brynberian, Crymych, Pembrokeshire,
SA41 3TN
07748 613444
www.firstleaf.co.uk

*Specialist grower of edible flowers, salad leaves, herbs,
microleaves, microgreens, cresses, peashoots and more.
Visits by appointment only.*

DAIRY

BLAENAFON CHEDDAR COMPANY
80 Broad Street, Blaenafon, Torfaen, NP4 9NF
01495 793123
www.chunkofcheese.co.uk

*Eleven varieties of Cheddar and four varieties of goats
cheese are available from this specialist company based in
the World Heritage site of Blaenarfon.*

CARMARTHENSHIRE CHEESE COMPANY
Boksburg Hall, Llanllwch, Sir Gâr/Carmarthenshire
SA31 3RN
01267 221168
www.carmarthenshirecheese.co.uk

*Producers of Pont Gâr cheese, which comes in a variety of
strengths and flavours.*

CAWS CENARTH
Fferm Glyneithinog, Lancych, Carmarthenshire
SA37 0LH
01239 710432
www.cawscenarth.co.uk

*Artisan cheesemaker and winner of Supreme Champion at
the British Cheese Awards 2010.*

COWPOTS ICE CREAM
Pen-y-Bac Farm, Cyffig, Whitland, Carmarthenshire,
SA34 0NG
01994 240434
www.cowpotsicecream.co.uk

*Natural ice-cream made with the milk of Jersey cows in
the Camarthenshire countryside. Their welfare is of prime
importance and their quality of life reflects in the milk they
produce.*

HUFENFA'R CASTELL
Capel Dwr, Castle Square, Harlech, LL46 2YH
07810 164547
www.hufenfa.co.uk

*Only Welsh milk and local cream, along with any number of
delicious whole ingredients for flavours, go into making the
ice-cream here.*

RACHEL'S DAIRY LTD
Unit 63, Glan Yr Afon Industrial Estate, Llanbadarn
Fawr, Aberystwyth, SY23 3JQ
01970 625805
www.rachelsorganic.co.uk

*Britain's first ever certified organic dairy and producers of
delicious milk, butter, yoghurt and much more.*

SANCLÊR ORGANIC
Glancynin, St Clears, Carmarthen, Carmarthenshire,
SA33 4JR
01994 232999
www.sanclerorganic.co.uk

Fresh, organic, healthy Welsh yoghurt cheese.

DELICATESSEN

BLAS AR FWYD DELICATESSEN
Heol yr Orsaf, Llanrwst, Conwy, LL26 0BT
01492 640215
www.blasarfwyd.com

*This delicatessen offers a wide variety of produce, much of
which comes directly from the producers.*

THE LITTLE WELSH DELI
22 Clos Gors Fawr, Grovesend, Swansea, SA4 4GZ
01792 895377
www.thelittlewelshdeli.co.uk

*Award winning company based just outside Swansea near
Gower, specialising in quality artisan sweet and savoury
food.*

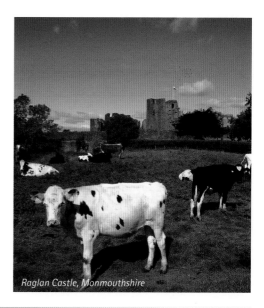
Raglan Castle, Monmouthshire

FARM SHOPS

GLASFRYN PARC FARM SHOP
Glasfryn Farm Shop, Pwllheli, North Wales
LL53 6PG
01766 810 044
www.siop-glasfryn.com

*Siop Fferm GLASFRYN Farm Shop was established in 2001
to sell the Estate's Welsh Black Beef, Llyn lamb, game, pork
and bacon direct to their local customers.*

M HUGHES & SONS LTD (GREENGROCERS)
Unit 4, Cae Bach, off Builder Street, Llandudno, Conwy,
LL30 1DR
01492 877963
m-hughes.co.uk

*M Hughes & Sons is a wholesale fruit and veg retailer that
is branching out into other areas so that they can now offer
their products and services to the public*

YEBERSTON GATE FARM SHOP
Yeberston Nr. Cresselly, Pembrokeshire, SA68 0NS
01834 891637
www.farmshopfood.co.uk

*Yeberston Gate superb quality, competitively priced Welsh
Black Beef.*

FISH

FABULOUS FISH COMPANY
01600 740646
www.fabulousfish.co.uk

*Beautifully fresh fish from finalists in the National
Seafood Awards, from their market stalls in Chepstow and
Monmouth, or ordered via their Facebook page for delivery.
A wonderful, simple way to receive quality Fresh Fish.*

HALEN MÔN SALT
The Anglesey Sea Salt Company Ltd, Brynsiencyn,
Isle of Anglesey LL61 6TQ
01248 430871
www.halenmon.com

*Sea salt produced the traditional way on the Isle of
Anglesey. Halen Môn. Available in an array of enticing
flavours and gorgeous gift sets. Today the sea salt is
enjoyed around the world by chefs and food lovers.*

MERMAID SEAFOODS & GAME
Unit 12/13 Builder Street, Llandudno, Gwynedd,
LL30 1DR
01492 878014
www.mermaidseafoods.co.uk

*Mermaid Seafoods in Llandudno, North Wales has, for
nearly a quarter of a century, enjoyed an unassailable
reputation for supplying the finest quality fish and seafood
to wholesale and retail customers.*

MEAT

BWYDLYN
01758 612136
www.bwydlyn.co.uk

*Welsh beef and lamb delivered straight to your door.
Bwydlyn specialise in courier and packaging to ensure that
all of the meat you purchase arrives in good time, next day
and as fresh as when it left their shop.*

CARMARTHEN HAM
Arfryn, Uplands, Carmarthen, Carmarthenshire
SA32 8DX
01267 237 687
www.carmarthenham.co.uk

*All of the hams are cured by Chris & Ann Rees at their home
and they intend to stay as a cottage industry and keep it a
premium product.*

DOUGLAS WILLIS BUTCHERS
9 The Parade, Cwmbran, Gwent NP44 1QR
01633 482436
www.douglaswillis.co.uk

*Since 1940 the Willis family have been producing the finest
meat, from animals cared for in the best conditions on the
hills of South Wales.*

EDWARDS OF CONWY LTD
18 High Street, Conwy, LL32 8DE
01492 592443
www.edwardsofconwy.co.uk

*Edwards of Conwy is a traditional, European award
winning, master butcher located in the historical town of
Conwy, North Wales.*

EYNON'S
Deganwy, Pentre Rd, St.Clears, Carmarthenshire,
SA33 4LR
0800 731 5816
www.eynons.co.uk

Family Butcher in St Clear's near Carmarthen.

GOWER SALT MARSH LAMB
Weobly Castle Farm, Llanrhidian, Gower, SA3 1HB
01792 390012
www.gowersaltmarshlamb.co.uk

Families have been farming the marsh by Weobley Castle
for nearly half a century. Their lamb is available between
the months of July and December.

THE WELSH VENISON CENTRE
Middlewood Farm, Bwlch, Brecon Powys, LD3 7HQ
01874 730929
www.welshvenisoncentre.co.uk

A family firm run. Andrew and his wife Elaine produce
venison using the highest standards of animal husbandry.

PRESERVES, RELISHES, HONEY & PUDDINGS

CHEF ON THE RUN FOODS
The Old Stables Tea Rooms, Bear Street, Hay on Wye
HR3 5AN
01497 821557
www.chefontherunfoods.co.uk

Award winning preserves.

GOETRE FARM PRESERVES
Goetre Isaf, Caerdeon, Barmouth, Gwynedd,
LL42 1DZ
01341 281422
www.goetrefarmpreserves.co.uk

Goetre Farm Preserves is a small Welsh farm preserves
business based in Barmouth, Gwynedd. Passionately run by
Karen and David Collett, Goetre Farm supplies high quality
Jams, Sauces, Chutneys and more!

SMOKED FOODS

BLACK MOUNTAINS SMOKERY
Elvicta Estate, Crickhowell, Powys,
NP8 1DF
01873 811566
www.smoked-foods.co.uk

Jo and Jonathan headed home to the UK in 1995 after
nearly a decade spent in Southern Africa, their thoughts
turned to Wales and the beautiful 16th century Welsh Long
House where Jo had spent much of her youth.

LLANDUDNO SMOKERY
Builder Street West, Llandudno, Conwy,
LL30 1HH
01492 870430
www.thesmokery.co.uk

Twenty five years of experience has taught Llandudno
Smokery how to source the freshest and best quality
products to supply to their extensive customer list. They
also produce a unique range of quality SMOKED foods (all
smoked over Welsh oak).

Three Cliffs Bay, Swansea

1861

Cross Ash, Abergavenny, South Wales NP7 8PB
0845 388 1861
01873 821 297
www.18-61.co.uk

THE BEAUFORT RAGLAN

High Street, Raglan Village, Monmouthshire NP15 2DY
01291 690 412
www.beaufortraglan.co.uk

THE BELL AT SKENFRITH

Skenfrith, Monmouthshire NP7 8UH
01600 750 235
www.skenfrith.co.uk

THE CASTLE HOTEL

Kings Road, Carmarthenshire SA20 0AP
01550 720 343
www.castle-hotel-llandovery.co.uk

THE CHECKERS

Broad Street, Montgomery, Powys SY15 6PN
01686 669 822
www.thecheckersmontgomery.co.uk

THE CROWN AT CELTIC MANOR

The Celtic Manor Resort, Coldra Woods, Newport, South Wales
NP18 1HQ
01633 410 262
www.crown.celtic-manor.com

THE CROWN AT WHITEBROOK

Whitebrook, near Monmouth, Monmouthshire NP25 4TX
01600 860 254
www.crownatwhitebrook.co.uk

THE FELIN FACH GRIFFIN

Felin Fach, Brecon LD3 0UB
01874 620 111
www.felinfachgriffin.co.uk

GLIFFAES COUNTRY HOUSE HOTEL

Crickhowell, Powys NP8 1RH
01874 730 371
www.gliffaeshotel.com

THE HAND AT LLANARMON

Llanarmon Dyffryn Ceiriog, Ceiriog Valley, Llangollen
LL20 7LD
01691 600 666
www.thehandhotel.co.uk

THE HARDWICK

Old Raglan Road, Abergavenny, Monmouthshire
NP7 9AA
01873 854 220
www.thehardwick.co.uk

THE IMPERIAL HOTEL

The Promenade, Llandudno, LL30 1AP
01492 877 466
www.theimperial.co.uk

THE KINMEL ARMS

The Village, St George, Nr Abergele, Conwy LL22 9BP
01745 832 207
www.kinmelarms.co.uk

MAES YR HAF

Parkmill, Swansea SA3 2EH
01792 371 000
www.maes-yr-haf.com

MANORHAUS

Restaurant-with-Rooms, Well Street, Ruthin, Denbighshire
LL15 1AH
01824 704 830
www.manorhaus.com

MIMOSA KITCHEN AND BAR

Mermaid Quay, Cardiff Bay CF10 5BZ
029 2049 1900
www.mimosakitchen.co.uk
www.mimosacegin.co.uk

THE NEWBRIDGE ON USK

Tredunnock, Usk, South Wales NP15 1LY
01633 410 262
www.newbridgeonusk.co.uk

THE OLD RECTORY

Country Hotel & Golf Club, Llangattock, Crickhowell, Powys
NP8 1PH
01873 810 373
www.rectoryhotel.co.uk

PLAS BODEGROES

Pwllheli. Gwynedd. North Wales LL53 5TH
01758 612 363
www.bodegroes.co.uk

THE QUEEN'S HEAD

Glanwydden, Conwy LL31 9JP
01492 546 570
www.queensheadglanwydden.co.uk

SEAVIEW RESTAURANT

Market Lane, Laugharne, Carmarthen, Dyfed
SA33 4SB
01994 427 030
www.seaview-laugharne.co.uk

SOSBAN

North Dock, Llanelli, Carmarthenshire SA15 2LF
01554 270 020
www.sosbanrestaurant.com

THREE SALMONS HOTEL

Bridge Street, Usk, Monmouthshire NP15 1RY
01291 672 133

www.threesalmons.co.uk

TY MAWR MANSION
COUNTRY HOUSE HOTEL

Cilcennin, Lampeter, Ceredigion SA48 8DB
01570 470 033
www.tymawrmansion.co.uk

TYDDYN LLAN

Llandrillo, nr. Corwen, Denbighshire, North Wales LL21 0ST
01490 440 264
www.tyddynllan.co.uk

THE WALNUT TREE

Llanddewi Skirrid, Abergavenny, Monmouthshire
NP7 8AW
01873 852 797
www.thewalnuttreeinn.com

Y POLYN

Capel Dewi, Carmarthenshire SA32 7LH
01267 290 000
www.ypolynrestaurant.co.uk

YE OLDE BULLS HEAD INN

Castle Street, Beaumaris, Anglesey LL58 8AP
01248 810 329
www.bullsheadinn.co.uk

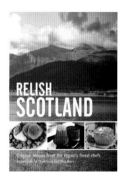

MORE QUALITY RECIPE BOOKS
AVAILABLE FROM THIS PUBLISHER

Relish Scotland – With over 300 Pages of Scotland's finest recipes, this book takes you on an epic journey from Edinburgh to Glasgow, across to Aberdeen and then up to the Highlands and Islands, through rugged landscapes and beautiful cities. An introduction from TV celebrity chef Nick Nairn prepares the palate for recipes from nationally acclaimed restaurateurs such as Tom Kitchin, Martin Wishart and Geoffrey Smeddle. With breathtaking pictures of the views and venues, Relish Scotland promises to make for fascinating reading for both foodies and tourists alike.

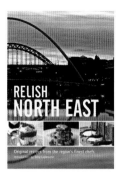

Relish North East – From the bustling city life in Newcastle, to the multitude of sleepy, rural villages, the North East has something for everyone. An introduction from the North East's best known chef, Terry Laybourne, kicks off this culinary adventure through a rich and diverse region, with many varied recipes for you to try at home including a selection from the North East's two Masterchef finalists, John Calton and David Coulson, plus many others from award-winning chefs across the region.

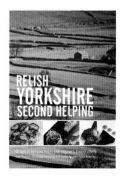

Relish Yorkshire Second Helping – The latest edition of relish Yorkshire features a foreword by celebrity chef Tessa Bramley, and returns to the county with all new recipes from Yorkshire's greatest chefs; Michelin-Starred James McKenzie from The Pipe and Glass and Steve Smith from The Burlington, plus Richard Allen from The Fourth Floor at Harvey Nichols and many, many more. Relish Yorkshire: Second Helping is a must have for any hearty food lover with true Yorkshire pride.

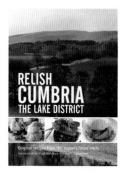

Relish Cumbria – Over 50 mouth-watering exclusive recipes for you to try at home from some of Cumbria's finest Country House Hotels and acclaimed restaurants including Nigel Mendham at The Samling, Russell Plowman at Gilpin Lodge Hotel and Andrew McGeorge at Rampsbeck Country House Hotel. Packed with innovative recipes and stunning photography to match the stunning landscape, Relish Cumbria is certain to make a fantastic addition to any cook's library.

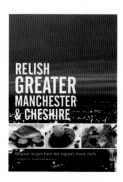

Relish Greater Manchester and Cheshire – As one of the most populated areas in the UK, Greater Manchester has a wealth of talent to display. Traditionally seen as a historic centre of industry, Manchester's finer side inspires great chefs such as Andrew Nutter and Stuart Thomson to produce truly amazing food. Alongside this, Cheshire offers a refreshing change of pace. Further away from the hustle and bustle, its own character is reflected in some equally stunning cuisine presented by Michael Caines. This Relish book shows it all in this journey around the North West.

Relish Merseyside and Lancashire – As one of the most historically significant ports in the country, Liverpool continues to have importance to this day, by giving us all access to a world of high quality food, but there is just as much talent further afield, as shown in the stunning chefs we have chosen to represent Lancashire. Renowned local chef, Paul Askew, starts of this book by introducing us to some of the quality produce that this region has to offer, and how he is so proud to be championing an area that has many great chefs and restaurants.

Relish Publications is an independent publisher of exclusive regional recipe books, featuring only the best and brightest critically acclaimed chefs and the venues at which they work, all of which is showcased with superb photography. They also work with some chefs individually to produce bespoke publications tailored to their individual specifications. Since 2009, Relish has fostered a national presence, while maintaining friendly, personalised service upon which their small but highly professional team prides itself.

Proud sponsors of

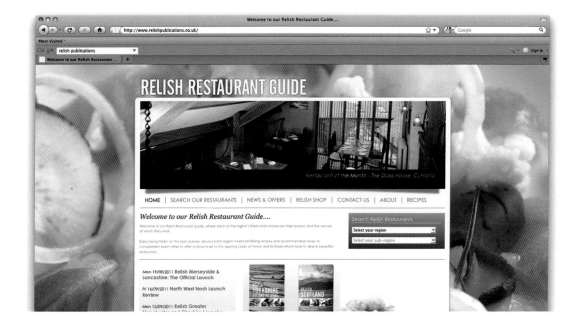

Looking to dine in the UK's finest Restaurants?

Simply log on to www.relishpublications.co.uk and find the very best your region has to offer...

The Relish Team has worked with all of the restaurants and chefs and have visited every highly recommended and acclaimed restaurant listed. These ingredients are what make the Relish Restaurant Guide genuine and unique. If you would like to be taken on an epic journey to the finest restaurants in each region and if you would like to download more recipes or add to your collection of Relish Books please visit www.relishpublications.co.uk